under the birch tree

a memoir of
discovering connections
and finding home

nancy chadwick

SHE WRITES PRESS

Published June 19, 2018
Printed in the United States of America
Print ISBN: 978-1-63152-357-1
E-ISBN: 978-1-63152-358-8
Library of Congress Control Number: 2017959574

For information, address:
She Writes Press
1563 Solano Ave #546
Berkeley, CA 94707

Interior design by Tabitha Lahr

She Writes Press is a division of SparkPoint Studio, LLC.

dedication
for Mom, Tim, and Ann
and in memory of Dad and Tom

the birch trees

*I'll always remember the birches for as long as I live.
It's the silver bark of the birch, the lenticels,
and the height they grow to whilst remaining slim . . .
but they always remind me of home.*
                                    —James Roy Blair Anderson

Birches struggle to survive, their shallow roots testing the soil, tender leaves seemingly suspended in stillness but growing and maturing. I was not without struggles, beginning with my roots, testing my footing while branching out with growth in evolution of my years.

5

In my early years, I grew to know a particular birch tree, planted on the same plot as I was. I developed a kinship with its youth; I noticed this one's ashen white limbs contrasted with its scattered dark-trunked tree mates of stately oak, maple, and elm. Its delicate arms played in uncomplicated innocence, inviting me to circle around it. I am reminded of Robert Frost's reflections of innocence, carefree spirits, and evolving years:

I like to think some boy's been swinging them . . .
And they seem not to break;
though once they are bowed,
So low for long, they never right themselves:
You may see their trunks arching in the woods,
Years afterwards, trailing their leaves on the ground,
Like girls on hands and knees that throw their hair . . .

To a Tree

The time has come for us to move on
Let us nest that time in the
Bottom of the tree
To grow with each new branch
Letting our leaves bud with
Each new spring
The nest is our home, the branches
Our foundation
It is the universal home of God
For I am set in the ways of the tree
I am bound for eternity.

There's something about trees. My discovery started at fifteen, when I wrote this poem and realized I had a place in this world. My birch and I seemed to shadow one another over the years, and a birch tree sighting spurred memories when I sought to be at home. When I was among the unfamiliar, my tree would tell me I was in the right place as I remembered where we met, where we came from. Trees became a metaphor for living, a guiding symbol for finding home, and the beginning for my story. My tree had a purpose.

part 1

the birch tree

underfoot and in hand

On a summer Saturday morning, the sweet scent of cut grass signaled the start of an afternoon of play. For a chubby ten-year-old, the short lawn meant my wide feet were free to run bases in the backyard without tripping over a thick carpet underfoot. It also was an invitation to take a seat cross-legged, and to enjoy a respite without having to rock from side to side to scratch my legs and rear end because of grass blades poking me from underneath. But I never stayed seated; I was a walker. I would circle the house, starting in the backyard, continuing around to the side door and then to the front yard to meet a landscaped island of pussy willows, evergreens, and a black light pole stuck in the middle of the foliage. As I neared the final stretch, I released an unconscious sigh at the top of the driveway and greeted my birch tree. I noticed my buddy's fullness, a thick base with surfacing roots, and acknowledged any changes I may have overlooked since my last survey. A gentle touch to its peeling trunk was a handshake in greetings. Its bark never broke off when I stuck my finger through a smooth papery curl dangling from its base. We danced with long leafy branches connecting, hand in hand, while dappled light illuminated our stage. Connections were learned and encouraged in this safe place. My home was underfoot and in my hands.

One warm summer morning, humidity obscured the rising sun as I stood at the top of the driveway. Lending its shade, my tree caught my attention as if to warn me. I inched closer. With bent knees and my rear end sticking out, I squatted to get a better look at the curb encircling its trunk. I stepped to the curb into the dim spot, knowing if I could get closer to the ground, I could focus better. My once-warm body cooled, and goose bumps crept up my arms. I'm not sure if my reaction was due to my cooling in the shade or the ignition of adrenaline anticipating what was to come.

Upon closer inspection, I noticed the grass was damp and the top of the lawn moved with punctuated jabs in the air. I was startled; I ran to the driveway's pavement. With one hand on my hip and a finger pointing to the tree, I could only think the shadows were playing tricks on me or else my older brother, Timmy, was behind this.

"Come look. Quick!" I yelled. Timmy was washing his bike in the backyard, concentrating on details of the wheels' spokes. My urgent voice signaled Timmy to let his bike crash to the ground. He took off to the front of the house and stood next to me.

"What's your problem? What's wrong with you?" Timmy asked.

I pointed to the curious curb. "Look, look closely, there—the grass is moving. What is that?"

"Where? I don't see anything. There's nothing there." He moved his head from side to side to see as many angles as possible.

"But it *did* move, the grass jiggled." I yanked Timmy's

hand and pulled him down with me. "Watch." As our eyes focused on the spot, I touched the blades and gave the turf a gentle nudge. He looked closer at the base of the tree, over the bumpy hills of roots and dried dirt clumps and then to the grass.

"Wow, it looks like a hole or something. Looks like a hole's been dug out, not very big, and . . ."

"What, what is it? What's there?"

"There's something in it."

"What's in there?"

"Touch it again."

"No, I'm not gonna. We're disturbing it."

"I want to find out what's in there." Timmy was never one to hold back his sometimes-misplaced curiosity, an annoyance to me during my brother's little-boy life. His curiosity showed me he was a smart kid. My irritation was really disguised envy.

With Timmy's urging, I gave a nudge, and the hole filled. Something was peeking out of the dark recess.

"It's furry." Timmy said.

"Fur?"

"I think they're rabbits, babies. I think they're little bunnies in that hole."

"Then don't touch them, just leave them alone," I said.

"No, this is cool."

I knew Timmy wasn't going to leave this alone. He pushed me away, and I felt awful because I had made my discovery public, and with that I had put the safety of that spot in jeopardy. I would argue that I'd discovered it first; it was mine, and that meant it was my responsibility to keep things right. I pushed him back. "Just leave it be. Let's go." As we walked away from the tree, Timmy in the lead, I turned around to look at the birch tree with its young thin branches reaching for the sky. I stood in tandem and innocence with my tree and noticed its peels on the trunk were shaking along with its leaves, as if frightened by the intrusion.

I embraced my home, establishing my roots with every step, hugging its boundaries. I always returned to my starting spot, my birch tree, where it looked sensitive with its white peeling bark interspersed with gray bumps spread out in its niche. It was a provider of shade during the days of blistering sun, and, at the best of times, it let the sunbeams warm the house during the most frigid hours of winter's cold. In my adult years, a birch tree sighting was like spotting home, like an instant message telling me to be comforted.

My birch buddy became a first connection as I learned that the tree was synonymous with home.

roots

While recently freeing my life of closet clutter, I spied a gray bucket packed askew with folders and paper and other goods aligned on parallel shelving. I delved into the vessel with abandon and plucked a few files, ready to purge the litter. Inserted within the stack were large sheets of thick white paper, aged to tan and arranged in quarters. I held the parcel like a curious treasure in my hands before separating the folds to discover blueprints on the reverse side. I spread the poster-sized drawing flat on the floor and squatted to read the details of the reverse print. The building commissioner from the village had given his approval, stamped September 4, 1964, when I was two. My girlhood home was illustrated in blueprints.

Memories flooded my mind. We were lot #18 on Carlisle Avenue. William D. Murphy was the architect . . . three-quarter-inch Driftwood panelling in the family room, (*paneling* was misspelled) . . . Donley Brothers Dutch Oven Door in the fireplace, below the mantel. There were views of the inside including the basement and crawl space, but there was no attic. I was disappointed that artifacts of my

12

ancestors, accompanied by dust and cobwebs as telltale signs of age, would not be found there. Old family photos were few. Letters bundled by a single string revealing my family and their relationships were nonexistent. I wanted to discover a rich heritage, a connection that might have been squirreled away in a hidden corner of the basement. My fingertip was a magic wand following the thin white lines to draw a circle engaging the contents to life. I was no longer seeing empty space.

The blueprints unfolded in white print, pages turning to show detailed floor plans. I was in my childhood home where I saw rooms alive with color. A pink-and-green wall-papered mural provided a backdrop to the pink wrought iron kitchen set centered in the breakfast nook and made me feel like I was dining in a fancy café. A large floral print in shades of green on paper hugged the dining room walls. "No sliding on the wood floors, you're going to get splinters," Mom would yell to Tim and me. Socked feet were mandatory for speed to escape when chasing each other. Mom's statement was serious enough for me to stop, questionable enough for me to examine the bottoms of my feet for loose brown specs imbedded in the sock's white stitching. I resumed sliding all the way into Timmy after I'd confirmed there were no wood fragments. We were bumper cars, knocking each other off our feet, disabling each other's slide progress.

I saw Agnes, my mom's mother and the only grand-mother I knew, sitting in a black Naugahyde rocking chair in our family room in front of the television, watching *The Price Is Right* while peeling an orange and then placing the oily citrus skins in a neat pile on an unfolded white paper napkin in her lap. When I went near her, an orange fragrance bloom would engage my nostrils. On the second floor, a pair of twin beds anchored the master bedroom with headboards bumped up against a wall of Wedgewood blue-and-crème toile paper, and in the dressing area, double sinks filled a black marble counter. In the basement, a Ping-Pong table—used more for Tim's arts and crafts than for family table tennis—and Dad's drum set complemented the ends of the floor.

That two-story house invited sun to spotlight the right rooms like lights illuminating scenes on a stage, thanks to a decorator who created the perfection Mom demanded. The living room was a showroom with red carpet underfoot and satin-covered love seats in creamy white with crimson velvet piping at the seams; black velveteen accent chairs completed a social circle. This was not a place for children, and on the rare occasion Tim and I were invited into the living room, our rear ends would have to pass inspection to make sure the silken seats would not be smeared with peanut butter or chocolate chip cookie remnants.

And then there was my birch buddy, never failing to include himself in the picture window with his branches posing as an umbrella over us. My home was not limited to its exterior circumference but spread inside through all rooms and inhabitants.

My memories summoned me back in time to those places outlined in white ink on the blueprints. Chapters in my life were like doors blown open with opportunity and closed with setbacks by gusts of wind where outside forces changed their direction. I would create a place for myself no matter where a challenge sent me. But was my place my home? The house on Carlisle was my home because I had started there. It was my point of reference, together with my birch tree.

early foliage

For as long as I can remember, Mom did not like to reveal that she grew up on Cleaver Street because it was in a poorer part of the city. "Cleaver Street. Oh, that bad neighborhood." she'd say, conjuring memories of her childhood during the 1930s and '40s. Mom told me there had been no toilet in the house, and they had to use one outside if they had to go. The placement of the toilet divulged their financial status. When I was a little one, I would visit Grandma on holidays at the house on Cleaver Street. I thought the house was situated in a good place because I could visit my Polish relatives—Uncle Tony and Aunt Helen, Aunt Harriet, and my godmother, Bonnie—in their homes without stepping outside, for their apartments pocketed each corner of the four flats. I thought this comforting to know they were all together as family under one roof, one home. When Mom married and moved away from her brother Norman and her mother, no longer sharing the same bed with her, she awaited an upscale life in a fancy high-rise condo on Lake Shore Drive in Chicago, a stark contrast to Cleaver Street and her small apartment with no toilet. Her life had turned richer than she could have imagined. But then she had kids, and that's where it started for me.

I was born in the early sixties to a mother who thought that once you married, you had kids, whether you wanted them or not. "I wasn't ready to have kids," she declared, negating her devout Catholic tenet declaring the sacrament of marriage necessary for procreation. Mom said Dad wanted to name me "Victoria" but he didn't want the kids at school calling me "Vicky." "Victoria Chadwick sounded like a movie star," she said. Perfection became not only Mom's mandate for her life but also for her daughter's. So "Nancy" rang truer, and I was baptized Nancy Ann, and my birth certificate declared Nancy Lee. This discrepancy went unnoticed by my mother and remains unclear today. My older brother by three years, Timothy Hugh, however, experienced no name drama. I never knew what my dad thought about having two more kids after having Ann and Tom from a previous marriage to his first wife, Virginia. Maybe starting again with Mom was a blessing because he had a second chance.

Mom and Dad met at Henri, Hurst & McDonald, Inc.,

an advertising agency in Chicago, and married in 1957 when Dad was a VP of Advertising and Public Relations for Admiral Corporation, a television and appliance company and the agency's client.

Instant trauma and isolation struck Mom when she moved from the city to the suburbs after they married, because Mom was a city girl who relied on public transportation and foot to get her from North Avenue to the Palmolive Building and down Michigan Avenue. "I had to learn how to drive to get anywhere, and I was scared to death. I was living in the middle of nowhere with two small children and didn't know anyone," she told me. Every time Mom belted up in her new red Ford Falcon her nerves gave a jumpstart, instead of the gas pedal.

Dad took Mom, Tim, and me on an airplane—really a small propjet—in the late sixties, to Detroit to watch Dad shoot a commercial. Mom was a nervous wreck during the bumpy ride, cupping her hands over her ears while fidgeting because of the loud noise from the propellers. I, however, was on an adventure. It didn't matter if Mom was traveling by car or plane; as far back as I can remember Mom was usually anxious.

When Dad brought home a black-and-white headshot of a famous singer, he pointed to the photo and said to me, "Guess who that is."

I had no idea.

"It's an autographed picture of Glen Campbell," Dad said. He laughed. I didn't think there was anything funny about it. It was as if he was laughing at me, testing me, knowing I couldn't answer.

Throughout Dad's advertising years, he would always say he was responsible for discovering Kim Novak. Previously an unknown actress, she appeared in one of his commercials, and her acting career took off. I found Dad's humor and boasting uncharacteristic of the reserved and quiet man I had been accustomed to. Memories of the plane ride, recording studio, Glen, and Kim represented equal parts adventure and discovery of my mother's nervous states and my dad's chameleon-like personality.

I wondered why these memories of Mom and Dad stood out. Perhaps I expected Mom to be excited and happy with me when faced with new situations, whether a car or plane ride, but when I would see her anxious face, tension in her stiff body, and lack of a smile on her face, I was concerned that something was wrong, giving me good reason to feel that way too. Perhaps Dad's invitation to join him at work, to show and tell with a photo, and to reveal a personal accolade were his way of connecting with me, and I with him.

When I was two and Timmy was five, the family moved to the Carlisle house in Deerfield, a northern suburb of Chicago. Our four-bedroom red brick colonial was the unspoiled suburban backdrop in membership with other two-story houses which sat like gems on their velvet green lawns set with oak and maple trees and manicured hedges. Growing up, I thought my house was big and modern because it was new.

When I was a young girl, Mom insisted photo opportunities were best served when taken in front of the house's picture window. I obliged her because my birch buddy was near, plotted in the center of circling greens where it stood tall and arabesque in front of me, as if to say, *look here and smile*, when my photo was waiting to be taken on my first day of kindergarten. The tree's branches did not shade my eyes, squinty from the sun's high-noon rays. My pixie haircut was aglow in sun-bleached hair; my tanned body offset my navy dress, patterned in tiny white polka dots, with an appliqué of paintbrushes and an artist's palette in primary colors at the hem. A white Peter Pan collar mimicked the roundness I was trying to evade. But the dress was too small because the sleeves did not meet my wrists, and the skinny elastic around my forearms left an indented pink ring on my skin. My chubby feet were crammed into blood-red Mary Janes, whose straps Mom had struggled to pull just to the first hole on the buckle. Standing at attention with my feet together and my hands folded in front, I posed with my heels brushing against the yellow marigolds in full bloom. Connecting with my birch buddy made the irritations of a too-small dress and short-strapped shoes diminish as my buddy's arms welcomed a toasty blanket of sun overhead. The tree ushered a smile on my face and a squint in my eye on that Indian summer day, allowing my contentment to win over my physical discomfort. I was present with my house and my birch buddy. I was at home.

ella

Ballet and Brownies initiated my girlhood. Though my occupations were a short-term investment, I learned that working with others was intimidating and difficult as I tried to keep up on toe and in Brownie points. I dropped out of both ventures, but not before I reveled in wearing the pink-and-brown uniforms in membership and belonging.

I loved summer vacations. The months begged for idleness, overshadowed by excitement in the morning not knowing the day's offering. Mom signed Tim and me up for swimming lessons at Exmoor Country Club, where Dad played golf on Saturday mornings. But our fear of water became a hurdle to overcome if we were to get past the first lesson, let alone put our faces in the pool. One summer morning, the sun was warm and bursting out of a deep blue sky when we arrived at the club for our lesson. I sat on the rough ground poolside and resisted the coarse cement pull at my bottom. Rocking back and forth, the water and I fell into a rhythm. The sun's reflection off the white cement made me squint hard as I stared into the bright water, watching the ripples inch toward me. I became mesmerized by the visual chant distracting my sense of place as I looked deeper, hypnotized by the bottomless pool. Its depth fooled me. I was underwater. My eyes popped open, arms fanned, and I kicked my legs. I struggled to reach the top, or maybe I was moving deeper toward the bottom. I remembered the Catholic nuns at Holy Cross School telling me to be faithful to God when faced with hardship, so I yelled at him to get his attention fast and to invoke my faith in my savior: "Get me out of here! Where do I go?" I prayed to find my way to the surface. I heard my ears fill with water, and then I couldn't hear. Soon I found light. The light's beam had guided me to the water's surface.

I learned that nothing really bad would happen to me and that I would always be protected. I think that's what the nuns meant back then when their mighty voices said to always be faithful to God and he will show you the way.

A savior scooped me up, wrapped me in a towel, and rushed me to the arms of my unsuspecting mother, where we took to our chaise to let the sun relax our emotions.

ellie

A household aura, created by my mother's unending quest for perfection and a less than perfect me, made me nervous and anxious. The night before a school test was one of panic, and the day of was trauma. Test taking jump-shot my nerves, flushed me with impending doom, resulting in giving my stomach an ache. I worked myself up to the point that I had to be excused to the nurse's office because I wasn't well. The pristine white office with a tall, slender lady in a white dress and matching cap declared my malady official. The nurse instructed me to sit on the toilet for a while. When no results followed, she sat me outside the bathroom to wait until my stomachache passed. It never did, so Mom was summoned to pick me up. When I got home, Mom directed me to the bathroom. "But drink this first," she said. "It's prune juice." I'm not sure if I was better because of the magic juice or because I was at home.

Mom sat downstairs in the den penciling in the crossword puzzle and watching *Days of Our Lives* on television while I remained upstairs. The contentment from being at home relieved my ache. My home relieved discomforts.

allie

When I became a fifth-grader, the music teacher introduced my class to musical instruments. The teacher played the flute, then the trumpet, the clarinet, and finally the saxophone. He said we could learn to play these too. That night before dinner I waited to show the permission slip to Dad until he was seated in his leather chair and had his cocktail in hand.

"We had an assembly today. I want to play the clarinet," I told Dad. I spoke softly, hoping he'd had enough sitting and cocktail sipping to respond.

I was drawn to the clarinet's solid ebony wood trunk with shiny silver buttons, tabs, and holes positioned like a zipper, creating music with choreographed finger placement playing the right sequence of notes.

"I could be in the band that plays concerts." I wondered if he was listening as he stared at the slip. I hoped my optimistic, clear tone of voice would divert his attention to me.

After a pause, Dad signed the slip. I wasn't sure if he approved, though, because of his lack of emotion and reassuring words. I considered his signature on the slip as his communication to me. We were off to the music store the next Saturday to rent a clarinet.

I was to play a solo for the spring concert, and while I waited for the audience to be seated, my friend Lucy, the flutist, and I stood at the door of the music room and peeked inside. My excitement and sense of importance grew when we saw a full house. Mom sat with arms folded in her chair as her eyes scanned the audience. Suddenly, her head turned to us in the doorway, and the glare from her eyes to mine was the beginning of the end. She got up from her seat and rushed to the door. As she bent over, her face matched to mine, her heated breath clung to my embarrassed red face.

"What are you doing? You're so loud with that squealing and laughing. You need to be quiet," she said.

"I . . . I was just looking . . . to see who was here," I said. I was mortified. My outburst of zealous chatter had been too much for her. I considered how bad I had acted but didn't believe that being excited and happy just like everyone else was wrong.

My excitement deflated. Just when I thought well of myself as a solo clarinetist, her scorn blindsided me. As much as I thought she was going to be proud of me, she wasn't. After the concert, there was praise and pride everywhere else, but for Mom and me, there was a quiet car ride home. The silence was heavy with her disappointment in me.

My deportment lacked perfection, and I don't remember Dad even being there. My hope for earning my parents' pride disintegrated. How easily a child's enthusiasm and self-esteem can be negated by one parent's scolding and the other's absence.

When I got home from school one afternoon, Mom was sitting in her chair in the den, watching the Cubs baseball game on television and reading the *Chicago Daily News*. I plopped on the leather ottoman in front of her and waited for her acknowledgement.

"So, how was your day?" she asked. I hesitated to answer. Mom didn't usually ask me this, so I grabbed the opportunity to chime in with details. I welcomed her interest in me.

"Oh, okay, I guess okay. I did better on my math test than I thought, and the extra science work I did was collected. I thought I'd go bowling with Shirley later today. Her mom would—"

"You know, they just can't seem to get any hits today," Mom interrupted, her eyes still on the television screen. I had momentarily lost her attention to a baseball team.

"So, aren't you going to ask me what *I* did today?" she asked.

"Okay, so, what did you do?" *Maybe she did something special for Tim and me.*

"Can't you tell? Can't you see what I did all day long?" She waved her hand back and forth.

"What? What is it?" I asked, alarmed and frustrated. I didn't understand.

"The house. I cleaned the entire house, did all the laundry, and washed all the downstairs windows."

"Okay, sorry, I didn't notice," I whispered.

I escaped to my room to wait to go bowling with Shirley.

I never understood why she was so upset with me just because I didn't notice her spotless windows and empty laundry bins. I thought every mom worked like this to achieve the same domestic results Mom did. I reasoned I was just a kid and it was adult, mom stuff. But then I realized moms don't get gold stars in recognition for outstanding achievement like I did when I'd ace a spelling test. I had failed to give her a gold star.

My only consistent companion, Martha, my school pal since kindergarten, lived in the corner red brick house up the street. We would ride our twin green Schwinn bikes with matching green-and-white baskets up Deerfield Road to Holy Cross School. The crossing guard at the traffic light considered us sisters because we looked alike with matching short pixie haircuts, round faces, and chubby torsos. I think I was considered the thirteenth child and an interloper to her family of twelve.

Once when Martha was at my house after school, we went upstairs to watch television in my parents' bedroom.

"Can we be in here?" Martha asked. She hesitantly put one foot through the doorway. I understood her reluctance to follow me because no friends were allowed upstairs at her house.

"Yes, I'm here all the time, doing stuff or just watching TV."

"It's a big room, and with a television too?" she said. "There're two beds in here, like that show on TV with the Petries. They're not together?" I noticed her wide-eyed expression as she got to see the bedroom of her friend's parents.

I didn't consider the question, let alone the answer. It was just something that was.

Mom and Dad weren't in their bedroom much—together. Dad waited for Mom to shower and dress, and then it was Dad's turn. In the dressing area, the double sinks never appeared to be occupied at the same time, and their closets were on opposite sides. A nightstand separated the two single beds. Splits and opposites characterized their room.

There was something about being upstairs in my parents' bedroom, though. A chair and television accompanied each other in the corner, and there was enough floor space for me to occupy in front of the screen to watch Andy Hardy movies. I napped on Mom's bed after my hot dog lunch on a Saturday afternoon when Mom was getting her hair done and Grandma stayed with me. Weekend afternoons and hours after school were spent in their bedroom where it was quiet, and I was alone. It was a covert way to connect to Mom and Dad through their bedroom and personal space. The open cover of Mom's vanity invited me to touch a few of her many telltale items. Peeking at her lipstick tubes, I discovered her favorite colors, how she made her nails indeed shine—like the bottle said—like cotton candy, and the wide-toothed comb that explained how she kept her permed hair in its round shape. Dad's vanity tray atop his dresser was simply displayed with just enough space for his watch, bracelet, and billfold. There was nothing more; it was just as unrevealing as he was.

Sitting in Mom's corner chair, I would look out the window to see the tips of my birch buddy below, as it stretched to reach my face. I had greeted its waving branches in contentment. My comfortable familiar surrounded me.

The summer days were long, and the nights hung on until the sun dipped in our backyard and for many more yards thereafter, illuminating the horizon with splashes of pink and golden yellow against darkness that signaled time to squeeze more out of the day. I would pedal my bike along the streets with speed in tandem with the night's fall, reciting who lived in each house and extending my home's boundaries. Darkness pushed the day's dawn into the earth. Coasting along Carlisle nearing home, I saw my birch tree signal me like a beacon with its top branches, young and sprouting, tickling the roof. I walked into a warm home from the cool night air and retreated to my bedroom, where I stayed awake until I heard Timmy's bedroom door click shut, well after dark.

one with Julia, and all that jazz

I thought Mom was good at what she did in our home. From her clever use of vinegar to wash windows and newspaper to dry them, to ironing bed sheets and Dad's boxers, I noticed her hard work and her sweaty brow. Perhaps one of Mom's most dedicated housewifely duties was cooking and being one with Julia—Child, that is. Watching Julia on television was as regular a practice for Mom as going to Mass on Saturday nights as a family. Julia was perfection, and Mom strove to be one with her because of that, even when she fell short. "This is not how it turned out for Julia," she'd say, standing over the stove.

Mom often referred to her *Good Housekeeping Cookbook*, a treasured wedding shower gift in the early fifties, which reflected its use with grease stains, stuck pages, and torn binding. Even though her menus were redundant, especially on Friday nights, she saw the elegance in a fillet of sole, Le Sueur's (the only acceptable, tender pea), and rice (required to be fluffy), even if Tim and I never noticed the details in her cooking or her perfectionism, which she consistently demonstrated on a plate.

Once, enthusiastic for culinary innovation, Mom gave Hamburger Helper a try when it was first invented. It was as if she had found a new recipe on a clean, unread page of her faithful cookbook. I stood by her in anticipation while she read each step from the box. However, upon first sight of the creation, she knew she couldn't possibly serve the gray blob. We shared the same adventure with trying to turn dried stuff in a box into a moist meal in a pan.

I reflect on these domestic practices and see how much they have influenced my own. I have my mother to thank for the understanding of cooking my own box-less meals, cleaning my windows twice a year, and washing clothes once a week. These practices are more than just learned; they are connections I carry with me today.

Mom believed in the value of preparing three meals a day, from scratch, and Timmy and I as young ones never felt neglected because of the availability of food. "Oh, what a happy, fat baby you were. So cute. You kept eating as along as Mrs. Butterwick fed you," Mom said to me. "She helped me after you were born, while my leg was still in a cast. She was always cooking and you were always eating." Mom thought if you were fat, you must be happy—and cute.

During one yearly checkup, when I was entering fifth grade, Dr. Kaplan said, "Let's talk about going on a diet." He showed me an illustrated pyramid with food groupings and what to eat as you went up the pyramid. I didn't get it. It was too complicated, and Mom wasn't going to be bothered with following a chart when her home-cooked meals sufficed for the family diets. So the chubby kids ate, and as long as we continued to do so, Mom would dish it up.

Oddly, my mother didn't think there was anything necessarily wrong with my plumpness; she considered it a mere flaw in me that could be corrected with a catalog. She reasoned to work with what she had, a chubby girl, and let the department store Montgomery Ward solve the issue. At the start of each school year, arguments would ensue at the sight of a new catalog in the mailbox.

"But why do I always have to get clothes from here?" I'd say.

"Because you don't fit into anything anyplace else," said Mom.

Hence, Ward's "husky" clothes, available to those who required more of a generous fit. I didn't want to be dressed like I came from a catalog, but for Mom, masking any flaws with stylish clothes was a valid approach. So I wore matchy-matchy outfits that illustrated "perfection," such as pumpkin-colored, elastic-waist polyester slacks and top with cream yoke and knobby, gold buttons at my shoulders. These garments ensured I stood out from the other kids, not because I was chubby but because of my wardrobe. My clothes made me different.

I could argue that I was blessed with a uniform requirement for gym class. I didn't quite fit into the school-issued blue one-piece with snaps up the front, so I issued my own gym clothes: polyester purple shorts with elastic waistband and a navy T-shirt. One day, Miss McGuire signaled me from the gym's doorway waving something blue in her chubby hand like a victim waving a white flag in surrender. "Psssst, Nancy, here's your new gym suit. I think this one will fit you just fine," she said with a smile. She was excited that the discrepancy of an ill-fitting uniform had been cleared up, as if she had just fit the last piece into a jigsaw puzzle. I didn't have to be different anymore because of my uniform. This one was similar enough to be like the others. I had surrendered to conformity. I had indeed been blessed.

elle

Despite our battle of wills over my clothes and the erratic nature of our conversations, which ranged from heated arguments to calming words, I knew Mom was a dedicated fixer, working hard at what wasn't perfect in her home and with her kids. She was always there for Tim and me, as a provider of the basic necessities of life through her cooking, our catalog clothes, and a clean and tidy house.

By contrast, my early memories of my father are few and far between. I assumed there would be an inherent connection simply because he was my dad, but really, we were two people who always encountered each other as if meeting for the first time. Our silence and awkwardness about what to say and how to be with each other was palpable. Connecting with him in similar ways as I did with Mom eluded me.

My earliest memory of him was when I was seven or eight, and Dad would take me with him to run errands on Saturday mornings. I'd tag along as customary and quickly learned to associate Saturdays with taking care of one's home and personal needs, a practice I keep to this day. In the summer, Dad wore a light blue or yellow cotton polo shirt and polyester navy or tan golf slacks, readying himself for a possible Saturday-afternoon golf round. Our first stop was to see Rudy at the barbershop. When Dad and I would arrive there, Rudy was always ready for him. I waited, seated in a corner in a big chair, nonchalantly fingering sport sections of folded newspapers and other well-handled manly magazines. I wondered why it took so long for Rudy to cut a brief line of thin hair that grew like a horseshoe around the back of Dad's shiny bald head. But the real time-spender was on Dad's manicure following the haircut. Oh, how his nails were shaped and polished to a shine. His nails shined just like his shoes.

The center of Deerfield could be experienced in a radius composed of four corners: Ford Pharmacy, Deerfield State Bank, a real estate office, and the strip mall with Jewel, the grocery store, plotted to make a circle surrounding the town's corners. After Dad attended to his head-to-toe personal polishing, we were off to the pharmacy, the dry cleaner's, the golf pro shop to see Brian, and then to Deerfield State Bank to make a deposit. We ended our tour at the parking lot of the pharmacy where we'd started. I thought maybe sharing his to-do list with me was a deliberate action to say to me, *C'mon Nancy, you're with me.* But I wasn't really with him in the way that our shared time was more important than the errands that filled it. I think he was giving me something to do to fill my idle hours.

Dad had a lean-over walk with his head down, as if he wanted his eyes to meet his shoe tips with every step. By the time we completed the to-dos, I'd noticed sweat bleeding through his shirt from the heat and humidity already in full bloom. Back in the Cadillac de Ville, the air conditioning blasting through the vents gave us immediate relief. Dad would pause while still parked to lift his eyeglasses off his face, pull a folded handkerchief from his back pocket, and wipe his bald forehead, catching rolling sweaty drops before they hit his collar. He would then replace his eyeglasses on his nose, steadying them just right, and then start the car. I would wait for Dad to ask me something during this cooling-off pause; I didn't care what he had to say. The conversation would be a bridge, an offering, extending a hand to connect. I grew impatient and gave up on my wishful thinking. Our relationship remained motionless in the silence between us.

On Sunday nights, the wafts of popcorn I smelled while taking a bath intermingled with Camay soap, signaling time to hurry downstairs to the kitchen. I focused on the large pot of popcorn as Dad shook it back and forth on the stove in a rhythm, stimulating more popping noises. He would fill the different-colored popcorn bowls to the rim, and then dribble butter and splash salt to crown the bumpy mound. I grabbed my designated colored bowl and headed to the den to watch ice hockey on television. But I didn't want to watch hockey. I wanted to sit on the couch and watch *My Three Sons* or play cards or Monopoly—with him. I wanted him to be interested in me and what I wanted to do. We remained quiet with our attention focused in different directions.

After dinner I would hear muffled sounds of the big bands coming from the basement of the house. I descended the carpeted wooden stairs in my bare feet and stopped midway to see Dad sitting on a black stool surrounded by a drum set. I was sitting on the outside, looking in. While he fingered the vinyl stack, one of my favorites was playing, the 5th Dimension's "Up, Up and Away," inviting my spirit to wrap around me and, together, travel down the stairs to the basement. Allowing the music to take me as the record continued, I lifted my bare feet, glided to the next cement pole, grabbed on and twirled, dancing to the music within my world. I loved the music just as much as he did, and I could lose myself in the notes and beats where he felt secure. I wanted to have something in common with him, meeting him somewhere on his familiar ground. If he couldn't meet me, then I would try to enter his domain. Eye contact would be an invitation to share what he had, to be a part of his life—a connection. However, Dad never looked up. I focused on him, and he focused on his music. We stared at our objects of desire. Dad kept his head bowed in concentration, becoming one with the music as his fingers wrapped loosely around the wooden sticks, allowing his wrists to snap to the rhythm. The record player needle hopped as it read the fine lines in the black vinyl until it reached the paper label in the center. The music stopped. He returned his drumsticks to their place on the record-player stand. Time for me to go upstairs. I wanted us to share the enthusiasm that music brought us, but we failed at our chance to connect.

One night after dinner, I followed the music and stood in the living room's doorway as Dad stood over the console, reading a record jacket, tapping his foot and snapping his fingers to some jazzy sounds.

"Nancy, come here." Dad waved over to me. I blossomed with a smile and ignited a kick in my step. "Listen to this. Do you like it?"

"I do. It's got a rhythm."

"Snap your fingers to the beat, like this," he said, clapping his hands. Dad showed me the record jacket. "This is Benny Goodman. Here's a picture of him playing his clarinet. He plays wonderful jazz."

He smiled at me as we listened to the music together. I wasn't tagging along or sitting on the outside looking in or diverting my attention. But the silence began as soon as the music stopped. I had hoped there would be more to our chance encounter, but Dad left the room.

I never passed up an invitation to be on the red carpet in the living room standing next to my father while jazz records spun on the console or when he read a story to me after dinner while seated together in a wingback chair next to the front window, where a world reflected to us inside. I tried to win Dad over, following him around town on errands, grabbing my popcorn bowl and sitting on his lap, and using our mutual interest in music to get his attention. I strung short scenes together: some characterized by the silence of the room, others filled with sound, and this is how I got to know my father. We couldn't seem to connect as father and daughter the way I wanted, but if I linked all the scenes, I could begin to know him. Today, I park my car once and run my errands in a circle, all with deliberate steps in concentrated motion while leaning forward. I pop popcorn and eat it out of a colored bowl while watching football or baseball, not hockey. I listen to old jazz with bittersweet spirit while clapping my hands in rhythm and remembering where I got my musical talent. Sitting in a small, dark, jazz piano bar draws tears as I listen to the drummer's beat. I wonder today if he ever got to know me.

disjointed

Timmy and I were required to remain seated before dinner during the week until Dad got home from work and went to the bathroom to wash up, replacing a lingering work smell with the odor of a very dry vodka martini and a lit Tareyton cigarette. Timmy and I sat on the faded purple-and-mustard-plaid couch while directing our attention to Mom and Dad, who were sitting in their respective leather chairs. Dad's wee slurp from his martini glass and ice cubes pinging in Mom's old-fashioned stabbed the silence. Dad would peer down his bifocals at the *TV Guide*, look up at the TV, and take a martini sip and then a cigarette drag, in that order. The air in the room decompressed as he worked through his ritual of relaxation. I don't remember much conversation.

On the weekends, however, we were not required to sit in the den before dinner. With empty plates lined up in the kitchen, Mom swung around to the other side of the counter to get a better look outside, where Dad was issuing one last flip of the T-bones. A summer Saturday night meant Tim and I hovered over Mom in the kitchen watching her glide from table to counter to the front of the patio doors, where she stared at barbeque smoke plumes. She was assessing the timing, like a conductor leading his orchestra, cueing the components to create a meal, the end. The smoke engulfed the Weber, obstructing her view to determine if the steaks were done. Just as she was about to slide open the glass door to halt further damage to the beef, Dad would be piling the steaks on the platter. When the orchestrated symphony of kitchen prep subsided, still-ness blanketed the dinner hour. We sat for dinner. Our heads remained bowed as clashes of forks scraping plates and piercing salad greens in bowls punctuated the silence.

And we're off, I thought, like horses lined up in their stalls anxiously awaiting the sound of the bell and the opening of the gates. Dinner was well into play with first bites committed.

"Just leave them there," I whispered to my brother, trying not to attract attention.

"I'm not going to do anything," Timmy said.

"I know you're going do something, something that's bad."

Timmy ignored my comments, which made me angry. His lack of response was in defiance of me and my wishes. Dad's cough-clearing interruption, which always startled me but went unnoticed by my mother, followed a brief silence. He asked, "What on earth are you talking about? What must he leave there?"

"Nothing, it's nothing going on," I said. I wanted the talk to stop because everyone was learning my secret.

"She found this nest of bunnies in the front yard, and she thinks I'm gonna do something," Tim blurted.

Now everyone knew, except Mother, who replied, "Bunnies?" Her eyes remained focused on her dinner plate as she excused the discussion as traditional kid banter that did not involve her.

To calm my upset over the bunny revelation, I considered leaving the disconnected, staccato conversation to search for a distraction, either in the backyard or cruising the neighborhood on my bike, feeling the freedom to discover every street again. The familiarity of my neighborhood gave me security when insecurity in my home was exposed.

As I surveyed the dinner remains in front of me, Dad slowly pulled a Tareyton from the open pack in his shirt pocket, examined both ends of the cigarette, and lit one of them, taking a deep draw until the tip turned red-orange. I paused and stared at the flaming end, perhaps allowing the mesmerizing fire and smoke to calm me just as it appeared to calm Dad and maybe all of us. Then Dad snuffed the spent stub. His mind returned to the dinner table after succumbing to a foggy trance, signaling the kids were dismissed. The dinner circle was broken. Dad left the table to grab a toothpick from the cupboard to pick his teeth, one by one, until the wood splintered. He'd spit and then move on to perhaps having another cigarette. Maybe Dad didn't have much to say about anything because chewing, cigarette smoking, and oral hygiene occupied his mouth. We went our separate ways, scattering like cockroaches that rushed to dark corners when the lights went on.

As I stared down my driveway contemplating a bike ride that following Saturday afternoon, I saw Tim kneeling next to my birch tree. It looked like he was digging on all fours with his rear stuck in the air and his head plunked low to the grass. I ran to my tree and peered down at Timmy.

"What are you doing? Why do you have a box? What's that for?" My hatred for Timmy was grounded in pleading with him.

"I'm taking the bunnies to John's house."

"You're what? You can't do that. You just can't take them from their home like that. They will die. They're too young. Please. Don't do it."

He could not be stopped. He kidnapped them one by one and placed the fuzzy gray balls gently onto a pile of shredded newspaper in the cardboard shoebox. Tears welled; my voice shook. I cried.

"You can't do this. Stop. Put them back where they belong. They're not yours anyway," I said as he tucked the box under his arm and hopped on his bike. I followed him down the road with my eyes until I lost sight of him. I looked at the ground hoping to see furry movement, but instead I saw the den was empty; there was a black hole. They were so little. For sure, they would die. I had let my buddy down. I wondered if I had betrayed my tree by not protecting it from harm. I took for granted the giving nature of my tree as provider of shelter, an anchor to my growth.

My earliest memories of my house were of an idyllic place with a picturesque way about it, where I had established my connections from its very interior walls to its exterior land-scape, where my tree had provided a safe, secure place for the bunnies, where they had a home and I did too. But discovering the bunnies and their subsequent eviction by my brother imparted unrest and suggested that maybe my security and safety might not always be forever as well. I had looked through a new window, and my new vision became a fore-shadowing of changes to come.

silence

Tim's and my behavior toward each other began as traditional sibling banter. With lack of supervision, Timmy would entice me to sit with him on the black Naugahyde swivel chair as if he had a secret and I needed to come close. As quickly as I hopped on the chair, he would hop off, grab the back of it, and run in circles, spinning the chair. He would then stop, pull me from the chair, and laugh at my drunken footing caused by my dizzy head. I wasn't terribly upset; my laughter was clearly heard over my yelling and fake cries for him to stop.

But as we grew up, we grew out of our teasing ways. We no longer chased each other around the house or in a chair, but distanced ourselves to become live wires on a slippery floor, flopping and sliding in opposite directions where we found spaces within the confines of our own bedrooms.

I kept busy in my room with cleaning and rearranging my things, putting them just so on shelves. Potted plants of unequal sizes accented white tabletops. A small glass ball with a hole threaded by a thin plastic rope was hung over the lock of my double-hung window. The brazen sun enveloped the ball and took hold of the gnarly roots as they struggled to expand in their water-filled round bottom. The light filtered and refracted upon the globe into tiny rainbows. I smiled at the sight of rainbows on my window. I was in control of my small space where I wasn't alone—I had all that was me huddled in a space surrounding me, reassuring me of who I was.

As I grew, so did my interests and creativity, and the floor became covered with what was me. I would often sit on the yellow-and-white shag carpet and engage my creative mind, filling the silence that the closet walls, looming tall and wide, enveloped while my young self sat small and narrow in the middle of the floor. I surveyed its perimeter, spying an Etch A Sketch, a Lite-Bright, and a plastic briefcase containing art supplies. A large shoebox filled with crayons was nestled near the door in the corner next to my Singer Genie sewing machine. A macramé box was slid underneath an old canvas bag with knitting and crochet needles sticking out in all directions. My creativity spoke through my busy hands. In my bedroom and my walk-in closet—whose cave-like surroundings gave me security and inner contentment—I was not confined but comforted by the connections surrounding me and the chance to be away from the silence of the entire house.

These spaces became a petri dish for my development, along with the kids' bathroom, where I noted benchmarks of my growth. In the bathroom, a beige Formica counter ran the length of the wall with muddy blue double sinks planted in the long surface. And then there was the small window at the end of the bathroom with a plastic marble coating diffusing an outsider's view—and an insider's. The window remained open to varying degrees to allow a clear view of the outside to slide through. The outside, an intermingling of sounds, smells, and fragmented sights, was a connection as I experienced life's growth in the bathroom.

When I was a preteen, Mom made a full disclosure to me.

"What *is* that?" I demanded, watching her grab a contraption from the upstairs closet.

"It's a tape player. I want you to hear something," she said.

I waited as she laced the skinny brown tape from the plastic wheel through the track and picked up the end by a slot in another plastic wheel on the opposite side. She pressed a small lever, and the wheels started to move in sync. A tiny voice sang, and then incomprehensible chatter followed while a four-year-old was bathing. I was in my world, content and safe in the confines of my tub in the kids' bathroom. I didn't realize then that my outlook to the world was behind the dim view of the closed window.

When I became a student of kindergarten, I could sit on the counter while Ann, my older half sister, cut the bangs of my short pixie haircut. Mom would crack the window to ease my insecurity and nervousness while I steadied myself on the slippery Formica as Ann came at me with a pair of pointed scissors. Mom reasoned that the procedure would be effortless and speedy as long as fresh air from the outside mingled with the warm air inside. I agreed. I had passed the time by recalling my carefree spirit when being outside.

As I grew, the bathroom window was raised from just a crack. I would situate my growing body in the middle of the counter and hang my head over my sink—the one closest to the window—so Mom could wash my hair with Johnson's baby shampoo. The counter was hard and unforgiving, but not as much as the curve of the porcelain under my neck. The noise of kids' laughter and screams outside traveled through the window and comforted me as I looked to the openness, wanting to be out there. After I was towel-dried and combed out, I hopped on my green Schwinn and let the breeze take my honey-colored waves, turning my head from side to side, to smell the cleanliness tickle my nose, engaging in freedom with my three-speed. I had joined the outside.

Through the years, my reflection in the gold-framed mirror changed. I didn't want the outside to know I was in the bathroom doing private things, so I lowered the window enough to allow only a draft of air. When I was in sixth grade, daily images of my wide mouth, pried open with tarnished silver braces, showed my struggle to paste tiny squares of wax on the sharp points of the tooth-straighteners. And in junior high, applications of makeup—the silent smoothing of blush on my already-warmed pink cheeks and the delicate strokes of black mascara—transformed a cute girl into a pretty lady. But then I was back to the hair drama where maybe pigtails weren't right, so I let the bundled hair pair loose. Growing to maturity, I propped a leg on the sink curve to shave my legs for the first time, stroking the razor up my shin to create a stripe of silken flesh in the thick white foam. The newly tender skin on my legs made me stand no longer as a girl but as a young woman.

I stayed plugged into the outside, where the world kept moving at a pace I tried to keep up with in the bathroom. From my first years in life and a closed window to connecting to the outside through the raised window, the bathroom witnessed my developing identity. The kids' bathroom was a private place where it was just me, the mirror, and the outside.

ellee

While my connections to home continued to grow, Tim was cultivating his talents with music and art. His expression of intelligence and creativity unfolded with each strum of steel strings on his electric guitar and continuous sweeps of his charcoal pencil or brush of oil paints on canvas. A couple of his oil paintings were good enough to show in the art exhibit at school, but Mother forbade him to enter his artwork because she thought it was dark and depressing. "What would everyone think?" she said. Her answer was in the silence of no reply; the conversation had ended before it ever started. Tim's expressions were his avenues of coping with the noisy confusion in his head as he wrestled opposing forces—his talent and the disavowal of his special gift.

I didn't think much of her statement at the time. But now I realize how Mom's forbiddance negated the very opportunities Tim was awarded by showing his artwork.

Her judgment told Tim if his work was bad, then he must be bad, unworthy of being among the specially chosen. I didn't think Tim was bad. He just wanted to show himself to others and that he was like them.

Tim would announce his departures from his bedroom, the only place he occupied in the house, with the abrupt ending of the Rolling Stones, the swift opening of his bedroom door, pounding down the stairs with heavy feet, a hop over the last step, boom, with both feet landing on the hall floor, and slam, the front door shut. His actions were reversed after entering the house—pounding up the stairs, slamming his bedroom door, and blasting rock music on his stereo. The noisy drama never bothered me because, after hearing it regularly, the distraction became an additional part of the household landscape. Mom, however, had no patience. "Can you paleeese turn it dowwwn?" she'd yell while fist-pounding the wall next to the stairs leading to his bedroom. The music continued. Then it was Dad's turn—a harder two-fisted pounding. I then looked for cracks in the wallpaper as I headed upstairs after his music-ending request, as if to discover a shift in the house's foundation.

One fall evening, Mom and Dad were preparing to attend a fundraising dinner party. In the seventies, drinking and mingling were as popular as they had been back in the fifties, when Mom and Dad were dating, and people were still using work to get to drinking and mingling, and using partying to get work and secure clients.

While Mom remained focused on presenting herself for the evening, a priority she took seriously because she was going to be among people in a class of which she considered herself a member, I hopped on my bike for a ride down Carlisle. Nearing home, I saw the garage door open and my mother and father scurrying out of the garage as if they had seen some frightful vermin. As I rode my bike up the drive to meet them at the open garage door, I sensed something was wrong. Dad looked furious, his red face and tight jaw filling the silent air. I deferred to Mom for an explanation.

"We're not going," Mom said.

"What? Why not? What's going on?" I asked. Mom's declarative statements begged for more questioning.

"We have to cancel," she said. It was a crisis, I thought.

"We're not going out this evening because of your brother," she said. I picked up her dramatic tone and wondered what was so bad that they had to stay home. When I walked into the house my eyes locked on Tim, who wore a grin and a sheepish expression on his face.

When Dad appeared in the family room, he directed Tim with a pointed finger, jabbing the air: "Go to your room." I didn't need to say anything because a lingering cloud of sweet, stale odor was a telltale sign of what my brother had done.

My heart pounded, and my cheeks flushed. I had never seen Dad this angry; actually I had never seen him express this much emotion. Meanwhile, Mom was walking through the garage with her long sherbet-green-and-vanilla silk-and-taffeta dress following her rapid pace. The more she glided, the more the sequins on the bodice sparkled, enriching her perfection. She was headed for the garbage cans, holding at arm's length what looked like a long brown plastic pipe and other paraphernalia resembling parts for something. This was a picture of opposing forces: a dirty, smelly plastic thing clashing with her perfection in dress, coiffed hairdo, and made-up face that was so right. The four of us were like mice in a maze, making our turns—Tim to his bedroom, Mom out to the garage, Dad pacing the family room, and me standing in the front hall—and going nowhere.

The three of us stood outside Tim's room, regarding the violator and his accomplice, his bedroom where it was dark and cocoon-like with shades and drapes drawn. Dad and Mom didn't step into the unknown but instead shook their heads and retreated in surrender. I, however, never hesitated to step into my brother's domain, a dark abyss that did not appear to have a clear way out. But Tim had a way out through an open window atop the sloping roof that overlooked the backyard and beyond. This was his perch, his silent place where he could step out of life and away from the perils of being a teenager. Maybe sitting on top of it all made him feel in control when something out of control ignited in the house. I would walk into his room and scan his setup, touching nothing so as to not leave clues I had been there. Tim had a CB radio sitting on his desk, dusty from lack of use, with parts scattered around it. Record stacks bookended the record player, and speakers were strategically placed on opposing walls for maximum sound output. He had a desk that wasn't used for studying but provided more space for a collectible he thought was popular. And then there was some stuff I had never seen. It looked like something dirty from outside. They smelled bad.

"What did you get yourself into?" I asked.

Tim laughed. "Just got caught."

"I guess you've been doing this for a while, huh? Smokin' this stuff?" I said. My question wasn't accusatory but curious.

I had nothing more to say. I walked to my room and shut the door. The silence of the house seized my attention just like the familiarity of silence among us.

I sought comfort lying on my bed. The silence was cracking, and I became unsettled and insecure at the numbing the silence evoked. My parents' choice to stay home was not punishment for Tim but a dramatic act to instill guilt and fault because their evening had been canceled. Tim didn't think much about how his pot smoking was no longer a suspicion, especially for Mom, as she would notice the sometimes-putrid smell hanging in the air of Tim's bedroom, the crumb-like debris embedded in the carpet, and dirty sandwich bags hanging out of his nightstand drawer. Now her inkling had been confirmed. Tim's lighthearted admission and chuckling told me he'd simply gotten caught with his hand in the cookie jar, and it wasn't a big deal. I didn't think his transgression was as serious as the anger Mom and Dad were displaying. Perhaps Tim's offenses—unworthy artwork, smoking, and playing loud music—were adding up to be about a person our parents did not like.

Now I realize that the anger I saw in our parents was really a reflection of their disappointment in Tim. This bad thing that he had done added to his reclusive habit of staying in his bedroom with the door closed. Our parents were powerless as they saw Tim becoming not so perfect and clean-cut anymore. He wasn't becoming the person they wanted him to be as his hair grew from crew cut to shaggy lengths, and he exchanged his starched button-down shirts for outstretched novelty T-shirts, his ironed trousers for crumpled blue jeans.

When Tim and I were younger, our parents could control our veneer of perfection, well-dressed in a respectable image to match our well-behaved deportment as a reflection of their exceptional parental skills. But now the perfection was backfiring, and the resulting silence among us spoke volumes.

One Saturday afternoon, Mom and Dad were preparing lunch at the kitchen counter when I walked in. I blurted out my curiosity to break their lack of acknowledging me.

"Is Tim working today?"

"Yes," Mom said. My question did not distract her.

"Really? Well, I was riding my bike . . ." I lowered my voice and finished in soft words. "And I saw Tim's bike at Jackie's house." I realized what I had said was none of my business.

"You did?" Dad said, turning to my mother. "Just what in the hell is he doing at his girlfriend's when he's supposed to be at work?" Dad's anger erupted. "You get back on your bike and go to Jackie's and tell your brother to get home, right now," he yelled at me while pointing to the door. I blasted through the door. The sense of urgency made me ride my bike hard and strong, but my sense of protecting my brother held me back. As I rounded the corner approaching Jackie's house, I saw Tim's bike was gone. I rode in circles deciding what to do. I believed there would be a simple explanation.

Arriving at home, I parked my bike next to Tim's at the top of the driveway. I walked into the house to see Mom at attention with a hand on one hip and her other hand over her mouth. Tim and Dad stood close together. This pairing was unusual because no one in the house had stood together like this before. And I don't remember Dad ever looking directly into anyone's face the way he looked into Tim's. Our closeness felt contradictory. After we had learned to spend time in our own corners of the house, here we were in the same corner. The closeness said we were communicating, but the circumstances and their emotions broke us. We could no longer be close without being divided.

"Just what do you think you are doing? You were supposed to be working, and you were at your girlfriend's house."

Dad's face bloomed red, and he breathed so fast that when he forced the air out of his hairy nostrils, it sounded like horses nearing the finish at the Kentucky Derby. His jaw clenched; his eyes widened; I had never seen him so explosive. I thought he was going to have a heart attack, and he would have blamed it on Tim. As I watched his face, I spotted his hands forming fists. The louvered doors shuddered and banged from the force of Tim's body being pushed into them. Tim fell back, and the give of the doors cushioned him.

Tim remained silent.

"And . . . what . . . were you doing over there? Why . . . weren't . . . you . . . at . . . work?" Dad continued.

I didn't care about Dad, I cared about Tim, who had cowered and rolled his shoulders inward. His head was down, his arms bent, protecting his chest and stomach. He froze.

"Stop, Tom, just stop right now! No, no, don't do this, just stop it, that's enough of this!" Mom shouted.

"Young lady, you go right upstairs, right now, get to your room," Dad said to me. I couldn't leave. I needed to yell, to demand that Dad stop. But he didn't. Nothing stopped the flow of the anger that seemed to pour out of him easily, erupting with unrestrained punches. *I did this to Tim; I made this happen*, I thought.

I didn't go upstairs. Dad's reaction paralyzed me as I questioned whether this was really happening. His assaults subsided only after the yelling between his punches ceased.

I couldn't take my eyes from Tim's face as it bloomed red with fear, hurt, and sadness in his welling eyes. He succumbed to Dad's anger in fist and mouth while remaining hunched to protect himself. How could a father hit his child in such a rage? How could Dad have so much anger? I wanted the silence to blanket us, warming the chill on that heated day.

We were together in a strange way. When we tried to communicate with one another, we couldn't. Forceful emotions spoke louder than any usual chatter.

Tim and I retreated to the top of the stairs, where we separated to our rooms at opposite ends of the hall. The cloistered upstairs kept out the bad that had happened with the closing of bedroom doors. I didn't know what my parents were doing or where they were in the house. It was silent again, and the silence meant everything was okay.

Whether it was silence of the house or silence of the lips, the underlying noise that preceded the clashes still buzzed in my head. Tim and I stumbled into separate worlds, letting the silence push out intrinsic family connections. We became more fragmented, sliding in opposite directions. Disconnections remained steadfast.

a shift in the ground

"When's Dad coming home?" I repeatedly asked Mom. "Oh, I don't know, I'd have to look. Another ten days or so," she'd say. I think my question annoyed her because she was reminded of his absence and her being a single parent. Dad's itinerary governed us. His schedule, grouped by hard black horizontal lines on yellow lined paper, was organized by days and indicated flight arrival and departure information, the hotels he'd be staying in, and the cities he'd visit. Dad was prompt and thorough with his itinerary sheets. It was as if he were bestowing comfort to my mother that his whereabouts would always be known on any day. Looking back at this, I found that yellow paper was his permission slip, his alibi, his okay to be somewhere with someone else, other than where he should be—at home. It represented a way of life that we accepted as normal. Dad just about walked in the door when he needed to prepare for another business trip. "Hey, Nancy, can you please do some folding for me again? I've got the shirts stacked on the bed, ready to go," he'd say. He seemed happy about leaving, almost excited, but when he was home between trips, his mind was elsewhere, his lack of connection marked by his limited conversation. I hated folding those shirts, but I did it anyway; I felt obligated.

On the rare occasions when Dad was home, his presence was a distraction, when one would think it would be a welcome complement. Dad's snores and restlessness drove Mom to her own quiet spot—the guest bedroom. I didn't blame her. His snoring acoustics woke me up, too. A dividing wall was all that separated Dad's headboard from mine. I don't remember Mom and Dad ever being alone together in the same room. I'm sure they were, they must have been, but I never perceived them as ever being alone— together. Displays of togetherness—dinners out, anniversary or birthday celebrations, alone time—were not there.

44

They didn't even appear to be good friends because laughter, flirty cajoling, and teasing between them were noticeably absent. I thought their behavior with each other and with Tim and me was similar to the behavior of other parents. We just existed, really, never pausing to question how we connected with each other or whether the relationships among us were normal. We really had no basis of comparison because we didn't know anything different.

By now, I had finished junior high, and Tim was going to be a senior in high school. One autumn night, Dad asked me to come with him in the car to pick up dinner. I sprung to my feet, ready to head out the door in anticipation of being alone with Dad, a chance to have his undivided attention. How dark the night looked. Rain sprinkles on the car windshield obscured my vision, making it difficult to spot familiar sights along the route we had taken many times before. The night of darkness turned to the night of foreboding on the return trip. Dad pulled into the garage. He shifted the car to park and turned to me with a somber face. My thumping heart, echoing in my ears, cracked the silence. I stared ahead and braced for . . . something. Oddly, I was uncomfortable with the alone time with Dad when I should have been excited at the possible connection, a chance to be one-on-one with him.

"Your mother and I are getting a divorce," Dad said. I repeated his words in my head—his clear, succinct voice, as if he were getting ready to make a speech and testing the audio on the mike: "Testing, one, two, three, testing, one, two." I think he thought this was another exercise in public speaking, as he often did when making advertising pitches to clients for work. The words flowed out of his mouth in a strong, declarative manner without effort and without so much as a glance my way, a touch of my hand, or any other comforting, intimate gesture.

Oddly, I sat quiet and still, void of emotion, like when we first got in the car—just like him. My eyes remained focused on my knees. I didn't feel the need to cry or yell or express words of anger toward him. He had a paralyzing effect on me, as I recalled my numbness when Dad's anger had once spoken through his swinging fists at Tim. What was happening? Was this real? Though I had these questions firing in my mind, I couldn't shoot them out of my mouth. Silence won out over any chance of conversation.

I wish I could say that I saw a personal side of Dad in that moment when he had to be honest, that I saw an openness in him because the divorce had finally forced him to make his feelings public. But the real truth I had hoped from him, beyond the quick declaration, "Your mother and I are getting a divorce," never came. There were no more words or actions to show me his sadness, compassion, or regret as he uttered those few words.

Despite the lack of intimacy I shared with my father in that moment, I realized something else: this declaration meant that the "wrongness" of our family was coming to an end—an end that had a name. Though the mention of the word *divorce* sounded bad, the consequences of that word weren't. Indeed, I was relieved by the announcement, because an official declaration had been made, a final action that told me nothing had really been right about us all along. It validated that we weren't normal.

ello

When Dad and I returned home that evening, Dad followed me through the door. I saw Mom and Tim seated in the den, their stiffened bodies capped by dark faces where the lamplight glowed from behind their heads.

The night carried on as it had started: in silence. We resumed that which we knew. All four of us sat in our usual chairs at the table, where dinner was served from brown paper bags. Mom picked at her food. The rest of us ate as if nothing happened. Dad's back was to the counter;

Mom sat to Dad's left. I was seated on Mom's left, and Tim was next to me with his back to the sliding glass doors. I had peripheral vision—I could see the entire kitchen, outside to the backyard, and both doorways that led to the dining room and the front hall. I could see everything. And I did that night. It was the last time we would be sitting in a circle, together.

I had had no reason to believe Dad wanted to leave Mom, to leave his home, too. Also, I was young and didn't know differently about how parents behaved with one another. But now I know that something must have been missing for Dad—this is the only explanation I can give for why he wanted to divorce my mother. He wasn't getting what he needed from his wife and his home, so he turned to someone else to fill his needs. I wondered if he was ever happy with us. Mom remained connected to us through her actions by continuing her role as a stay-at-home mom who maintained the household while taking care of two kids and providing a hot meal every night.

Years later, maybe when I was in college or in my early twenties, any mention of the divorce was usually in one-sentence statements that popped up when Mom and I talked about how life used to be on Carlisle. When I joined her one evening to watch *The Sound of Music* on television, she blurted, "The divorce took me completely by surprise. And I'll never forget . . . while I was watching this movie in the spare bedroom. He just stood there and announced it."

"You had no idea?" I asked. I thought this was a polite way of finding out more details, when what I really wanted to ask was, "How could you not know things were that bad?"

"Not at all," she whispered.

"But the long absences, and those 'business' trips for weeks?"

"I never questioned your father about anything. We never talked. We never even argued. And that was a mistake."

I understand now how Dad's request for a divorce had

been a shock to her. She had trusted him and trusted that his absences for weeks at a time were for work. Now that her ex-husband the decision-maker was gone, her urgent need for attention was the beginning of everything being about my mother.

ella

I viewed my parents' divorce not as dividing time into "before the divorce" and "after the divorce" but as the line between childhood (before) and adulthood (after). Life before the divorce was lived each day like its predecessor. As a child, I didn't know anything different. I thought we would continue our lives as we knew them. But after the divorce, I didn't know what the next day would present as my innocence slipped away.

When Dad said, "Well, we'll have to sell the house, you know," I found this matter-of-fact, declarative statement mirrored his proclamation of the divorce decree when we were in the car. I didn't understand why the house would have to be sold. After all, Dad was the one who asked for the divorce, essentially a declaration that he would be leaving—not Mom, Tim, and I.

I became caught in the fray of splitting a physical whole—the house and all the things in it—and leaving what identified me and what I identified with. It didn't matter whether it was within the confines of my bedroom, what I held in my hands, or outside. It became my home, by definition as all-encompassing parts—my backyard, bedroom, parents' bedroom, basement, walk-in closet— and I needed to keep it whole. After all, these were my connections I had discovered.

I thought of my birch tree and the bunnies housed within its roots. The bunnies had been displaced from their foundation just as I was being uprooted from my home. I was losing my birch buddy, too. I would remember it as an anchor to all things under it, a foundation cradling innocence and nurturing growth, a protector, a guide and support with its bumpy roots peeking through the surface of the grass bed and its arm-like branches providing shade and enough sun to warm me. My buddy's glossy leaves danced in soft breezes with rustling notes playing to my ear. My home was my foundation; it was where I was from. I learned to understand that my birch tree and my home were synonymous.

ellu

I prepared to leave, to separate from the physical, my home. It was time to relinquish my backyard, tetherball pole, flower beds, patio under the maple tree with room for running through the sprinklers on steamy summer days. I had to vacate my room, bounded by cheery yellow walls that encapsulated my haven, my walk-in closet, a gateway to myself, the person I was learning to become. I concluded that I couldn't do much about growing up, but what I could do was pack all my memories and colored snapshots of what I had grown to know as my home.

My bedroom had evolved over the years commensurate with my growing years, where my young child self called tea for two to be set on a white table and chairs positioned under a window, and my preteen girlhood was more entertained by playing through stacked LPs leaning against one another on the floor with Bobby Sherman and Donny Osmond smiling at me from their record jackets. Dolls that Dad had collected from his travels around the world adorned one corner of a bookshelf. When I tired of seeing them and lost interest in conversing with my friends, I would wrap them in newspaper and pack them in cardboard tombs. Nancy Drew books, once standing at attention, would retire from investigating new scenes. Memories of lying sick in bed with the measles and a Timmy the

Turtle vaporizer gushing wafts of Vicks VapoRub–scented steam comforted me. The welcoming buttercup yellow walls provided safety I was drawn to and contentment I could count on. These were all my things, and my touching each piece had anointed it a part of my home. My ability to look at them in excitement and joy and feel their power as stimulating my growth was now in jeopardy. I feared losing the very connections that defined my home and, in turn, losing it.

Not only did I have to let go of the room I'd escaped to, created memories in, and found silence in as my friend and a source of comfort, but also I had to release the extension of it—my backyard, a bright world that filled my senses. I remembered a patch of dirt that was in bad shape with rocky lumps and hard clay. I'd tried to pound the dirt to soft soil, but the earth stood her ground and remained hard. I planted a seed mixture of wildflowers anyway, reveling in the ease of sprinkling the salt-and-pepper-colored magic dust from the white envelope onto the lumps and discovering green tips sprouting quickly. The dust turned to green dots, which soon formed leaves bursting through the earth. All grew to be different colors with a variety of blooms, including one tall sunflower that stood strong. It was the last flower to tower in the bed when the others had reached their end, shriveled and flopped on their sides. A pair of willow trees stood soft in the opposite corner with flowing limp branches. An all-encompassing oak tree in the middle of the yard spread in many directions and never bent in the wind. I sunbathed on the patio during the sunny, hot days of summer basking in the sun, skin slicked with baby oil, listening to the portable radio playing "Summer Breeze" by Seals and Croft with no desire to be in any other place. Gentle breezes roused the leaves' stillness; robins and sparrows chirped in conversation while I witnessed the unfolding of delicate rose petals in Mom's rose garden on rich summer days.

My physical, material world defined my foundation. Scenes were staged in each room, represented by four walls and props. These components were physical pieces that had been constructed and added to over the years to declare the entire story a home. Would I soon be homeless, losing my components, my possessions? If my material possessions were to leave me, my definition of domestic security and safety would surely falter.

elle

A few weeks after the divorce announcement, it was as if there never had been an announcement, and our familiar routines resumed as if nothing had happened. My question to Tim—*It can't be any different than it is now, right?*—was more of a confirmation. We were on our own, but hadn't we been on our own for a while? We'd learned how life was during Dad's lengthy absences, evolving from a party of four to three people, so when Dad was gone, there wasn't a notable transition.

The once-new house would never be as it was in 1964 when the foundation's thin lines drafted on blueprint were virginal. The floors would be released of their coverings, and footprints would disintegrate into the now-thin air. The furniture would be relocated to new rooms, and the inhabitants would sit elsewhere.

"4 Bdrm, 2½ bath, hardwood floor in den and dining rooms, large eat-in kitchen and living room," our "For Sale" ad read in the *Deerfield Review* weekly paper. I had mixed feelings—sadness, confusion—as I watched our things being taken away. These were my things, my furniture, my connections that defined home. I was embarrassed and angry that I was a part of something that was not my doing. When I arrived at the neighbors' that afternoon to babysit, Mrs. Schafer asked, "Oh, are you moving? I saw the moving truck parked in the drive and thought you were leaving."

"Oh, no, my father is just moving out. My parents are getting a divorce," I said, in the similarly clear and concise voice of my father when he announced his divorce to me. I had to explain what was going on. I didn't like the position I was put in and hadn't asked for, something that he had caused.

Dad already had a place to live and someone else to live with.

As I helped Mom find new homes for the barely worn furniture, she reminisced about when she had worked with the decorator to transform the house into a showplace of personal taste and elegance with each chosen piece. She had everything she dreamed of—her perfection. She added, "Your dad was a good provider. We always had everything we ever needed."

I recognized her reflective moments in her words, of the home she had built over the years, and her attempt at disconnecting from that which was a part of her. I also recognized how she could have spoken disparagingly about Dad. But she didn't.

I sat on my bed the night before we moved. My eyes followed the yellow walls that still hugged me, halting at the window, and then fixed to memorize the view. I replayed the familiar, and then I had to look ahead. I was starting high school and would be branching out with growing limbs, exploring unfamiliar destinations, and taking root in new places.

Like the bunnies I'd discovered years ago that had been plucked from the only secure ground they knew, I was being uprooted and needed to find a new place to be. I took comfort in the knowledge that my birch tree would always be my buddy, and I would also maintain my connection to it. Because of that, I believed I would always find home, no matter where I went.

part 2

yellow walls . . . white walls

disconnections

The house sold quickly, and Dad helped Mom to find a new place with her half of the money from the sale. She found a new townhouse on Pheasant Lane on the westernmost unincorporated area of town. One Saturday morning, Mom dragged me to our new place to decide on interior details. As she spread sample boards on the kitchen counter, I knew I was going to be pulled into something I had no interest in.

"Help me pick out paint color and carpet, and then there are the appliances," Mom said, pulling me closer to the counter and sample boards.

"I have no idea. Just pick something." I waved my hand in a futile attempt to quickly dismiss her request.

"How about this carpet? It's got flecks of black, tan, and brown within the beige. This would bring everything together, don't you think?"

"Fine."

"And what about the kitchen?"

"What about it?"

"What color for the walls? We could really do a nice color, something different in here. With the new stove and fridge, it'll . . ." Mom was letting her decorator instincts and her quest for color-coordinated perfection in all the rooms get the better of her.

"Mom, I don't know. Just pick out what you like."

"But I don't know, help me, what should we get?"

I didn't want to pick out paint color and carpet. I wanted my mom to make the decisions as I expected parents to do. I had bigger worries about starting high school, afraid of not receiving parental support when I felt out of place at a new school. I wanted a parent—my mother—to make it all better. I wanted her to tell me to not worry about a thing, but my concerns were not hers as she tried to make her concerns mine.

Still, I never gave up on being Mom's personal cheerleader, confidante, and supporter when it came to the biggest challenge she faced: getting a job. Though finding a job in the late seventies was as easy as flipping to the "Help Wanted" section of the *Deerfield Review*, Mom was her own worst enemy. "I haven't worked in over twenty years," she'd tell me. "I don't even know what they're doing in offices these days. Who's going to hire me at forty-seven?"

"But you've got all that secretarial experience from before you got married. I'm sure you could use those skills in any office around here," I'd encourage her.

"I'm just not qualified," she'd say. This was her mantra, an excuse to not even try.

"You'll have to do a résumé. Look in the paper. You don't know until you get out and talk to someone. You've got to start somewhere," I said, hoping to end it.

A few months later in the fall, she found a job at Brenners Stationary and Supply.

"I don't know if I can do this," she reported.

"But you got a job!" I said. I hoped my definitive statement in raised voice would snap her out of her attitude. I certainly thought this would be the start of good things, and I wished Mom thought so too. Back then, I thought parents could do anything with no problem at all. I didn't understand her self-doubt and defeatist attitude. But now I understand. There was an underlying emotion: fear. She was afraid of the unknown and of facing it alone, a working world of which she had not been a part for almost two decades. Mom hadn't been bothered with securing an income, paying bills, deciding if a plumber needed to be called—because she'd had someone else take care of her for twenty-two years, providing her with anything she needed or wanted. But now the provider was gone, and she would be responsible for these requirements as a single parent without her provider. She couldn't do it alone. The void had to be filled, and that void-filler was me.

Mom needed daily reassurance that she could do it. But what about me? I had the same need. I channeled my focus and energy into just getting up in the morning and getting to school; I didn't have stamina for the both of us. And Tim wasn't much reassurance, as he was off on his own and disengaged from his mother and sister. Some of those summer nights, Mom and I really didn't know where he went, but I figured it out when he came home one night, and I heard him throwing up in the bathroom. Surely he had been at a buddy's house back in the old neighborhood, partying away.

The next morning, Tim was standing in the driveway next to his car with the driver's side door open.

"Don't tell Ma about this," Tim said quietly. He was washing out his jacket with the garden hose.

"What are you doing?" I asked, watching him clean the inside of his car of what looked like vomit. I knew the answer to this question.

Tim chuckled and thought the whole incident was funny. "Just a little accident."

"I heard you throwing up last night. Are you insane to drink so much that it made you throw up? And god, you were driving, driving a car while drunk? What are you thinking?"

Tim continued to wring out his jacket while neither looking at me nor answering my questions. If Mom was never going to know about this, I figured someone had to yell at him for his bad behavior. When I assumed this role, I realized Mom and I had something in common: we had a knack for asking questions where we already knew the answer, setting up an assumed offender for verbal berating, a common action by a parent. This was just the start of the shifting dynamic among Mom, Tim, and me, where our day-to-day relationship became a role reversal.

ellle

I had hoped I would have my own space at the new townhouse, an immediate connection to a long-lost familiarity. But the contentment I'd needed from my new environment was not to be. Our backyard consisted of a concrete slab about six feet square, surrounded by grass and sectioned off by tall wooden fences on either side. Goosebumps scurried up my arms as I stood on the cement, feeling naked without the familiar wrapped around me. The winds snuck through and wiggled the fence slats. New saplings hung in uncertainty of how to grow or in what direction. There was no shade to provide an umbrella of stately, leaf-filled limbs seeking new destinations. No birch trees welcomed me to let me know a piece of home was with me. Where was I? This wasn't my home.

When I walked out the front door, the familiar sight I had come to know and rely on was absent. When I hopped on my bike, my tree no longer stood next to me like a friend bidding me safe travels. I wasn't feeling adaptable, as if I could start growing again and branching out in a new clearing just like the nature of birch trees. The earth beneath me was heavy and impenetrable as the concrete block under my feet.

I thought of the abandoned bunnies forced out of their home. I wondered if they were cold and afraid because their new place wasn't like their old one, the place where they were born, where they were from. I didn't know where I was or what I was supposed to be doing. My lack of connection to anything underfoot or to my surroundings made me numb and disoriented. I'm sure the bunnies didn't even know where they were. The newness of it all—my backyard, the house, even my bedroom—wasn't enough of a distraction for me to be excited. My contentment with being alone at home turned to loneliness and confusion in a new place.

The time had arrived to start high school. I attended an all-girls school, about a forty-five-minute drive from the townhouse. Tim delivered me to school in his lemon yellow 1977 Challenger my freshman year, arriving at the school parking lot with spoiler engines roaring. The noise level, increasing upon the car's acceleration, competed with the blaring of Kiss on the radio, which could be heard even with the car windows rolled up. Heads would turn to the source of the disruption and eyes would stare in amazement and disgust. "Careful getting out, don't burn your ankles," he'd say, chuckling. My ankles, close to brushing the shiny side pipe because of a difficult stretch for my short legs, cleared with nothing but a breeze to spare between the pipe and my calf. Tim loved his car because of what it did and said about him, and he considered his sister's discomforted experience a compliment on his prized possession.

Hopelessness won over one fall day at school as the divorce, the move to a townhouse, high school, and a changing season with less daylight and more darkness overwhelmed me. I failed a first-period Spanish quiz because I couldn't keep up during the oral test. I was lost, and I panicked.

After class my teacher asked if I was okay as I stood with my face buried inside my locker.

"Yes, fine," I said. I smiled as if to will strength to my weakened self.

"I just need to study better," was all that came out in a trembling voice.

I cried inside. I wanted to blast inside my locker and hide and then jump out like Superman busting out of his phone booth ready to conquer all. After class, my eyes welled as I walked on the bridge that connected the old building with the new addition. I was drawn to the floor-to-ceiling windows, meeting the light and openness as if the mirrors to the outside would release my feelings of suffocation. I stood in front of the window to succumb to the sunshine and the infinite sky that hugged me in secure delight. Wanting to get closer to connecting, I stepped next to the window, where my shoulder touched the heated glass. I tilted my head back, yearning for calm from the sun's warmth. My tears continued as I stared at the heavens. I turned, exposing my whole self to the outside, offering my back to the inside so no one would see me. Aches started in my heart and spread to each limb as my emotions caught up with my physical pains. I wanted to escape, to will myself out of where I was, out of the time I was living in—hoping to be transported to a place where I was lighter and could be lifted above all the darkness that surrounded me, outside where a sky looked endless and warmth never ceased. I was void of a bond of being in a home, a home that had a birch buddy and a bedroom with a big closet that held a cornucopia of my interests and talents, a home where I was happy and safe. I envisioned soft cottony clouds holding me wrapped in a blanket of cheery sun.

The bell rang.

Once again, I evoked my faith and prayer skills I was continually taught in the Catholic tradition to be one with the Lord, asking him to help me make it through just one more day with grace and patience. It didn't work.

elle

Late fall had turned to early winter. Darkness loomed when it was time to go to school and had returned when it was time to head home. It was just about 5:30 p.m. one weeknight, and I was doing homework upstairs.

"I'm home. Where are you?" Mom yelled. I met her at the bottom of the stairs.

"It's dark in here. Why haven't you turned the lights on?" she said as she flew through the dark living room to find the light switches. The tone of her words pointed out my irresponsibility.

"I was upstairs, doing my homework. I didn't realize the time." This wasn't a satisfactory explanation.

"You mean you haven't started dinner yet? It's late; why haven't you gotten it ready?"

I could only stand in the dim hallway and join the silence of the house.

"I can't believe you haven't done this yet. I've worked a hard day, and I'm tired," she said, pulling the drapes closed.

Mom wasn't interested in my day. She didn't want to know that I had hours of homework, didn't have a friend to call for help, and that every day at school was a struggle. She was blind to my presence on the brink of falling apart from being sucked into an adult world that was all about her. I defied the questioning and rapid-fire commentary and remained unresponsive.

elle

As the cold of early winter seeped into the house, chills spread through my body when I ascended the carpeted stairs to the townhouse's second floor. I shivered there during that first winter when cold, drafty air from a wall of sliding windows met me whenever I entered my bedroom. The north-facing windows frosted over at times, and my hands would turn numb when pressed against the white walls. A grayish-white glow of ice crystals formed at the bottom of the windows, creating a crusty, tingly seal overnight to be discovered when I woke before dawn. My new room was cold and raw, like the outside, like the way I felt. My new place wasn't like the one I'd come from. The warm and buttery yellow walls that once surrounded me had turned to dull white.

When Mom walked into the house after work one night, she thought something wasn't right.

"Nancy, go check the thermostat and see what the temperature is in here. It's cold."

I scurried into the living room.

"Sixty-two degrees," I said.

"Well, what is it set at?"

"Looks like seventy."

"But it's not warm in here. It's on, but it's not heating in here. Now what do we do?" Mom screamed.

"God, I don't know, how about calling a repair person who fixes furnaces?" I yelled. "Who do you think fixes heaters?"

I was battling yet another domestic issue, one I believed was not my problem to resolve. Homework, long commutes to and from school, home obligations, and Mom's anxiety over anything new to her resulted in shared anger that put us in the boxing ring to endure verbal punches, leaving us exhausted.

Grocery shopping together was an exercise in madness. Public arguments might have been avoided if we had arrived at the store with a better-prepared shopping list. One day, when it was time to pay at the checkout, she barked, "What did you do with the checkbook?"

"I don't have the checkbook. You should have it," I said.

Her nerves were about to explode, resulting in an unfavorable outcome for me. Perhaps my red face and silence reflected my mortification. It was my fault I hadn't prepared a complete grocery list and didn't remember the checkbook. I feared that I could never do enough for her, that I could never do anything right.

Her expected life of perfection in her home—and with herself and even her children—was no longer perfect. Her dream house was gone. She was alone and in fear of the unknown, of having to learn something new, of a new house on a new street with new people, and of getting a job. Fear was the roadblock that prevented her from moving forward, gaining confidence, and living a new life of personal growth and opportunity, finding comfort and stability in perfection once again. My mother and I were both afraid, but sharing this emotion didn't connect us; it separated us further.

I can see now how this was her way of holding on to simplicity, the dependability of each day a copy of the previous with the familiarity of routine. I didn't want to let go of my past connections either. I wanted to keep my links and plug them into a different place, this place, here, now. I wanted to transfer my backyard on Carlisle, with its open space of green lawn stretching like a carpet, to the parking lot I saw when I looked out my new bedroom window. The lot would be my blank canvas where I could link to my past. I was without a home because I had lost my familiar; I couldn't find footing in this unfamiliar place. As with our days on Carlisle where lack of conversation limited our involvement in one other's lives, mutual support was nonexistent, and we scattered in silence into the unknown. The three of us existed separately.

under the birch tree

My freshman year was Tim's last year of high school. Graduation would grant him the freedom he needed from his emotions, marked by punched doors, drinking, and smoking during his high school years.

When the time came to commemorate graduation with a family photo, Mom poked her head into the family room while Tim was seated in the recliner, sipping a beer.

"You changed already, and we didn't take any pictures. Can you please put your suit back on so we can take some pictures? Your father will be here shortly."

"What? You're kiddin'? Not now, it's over." Oh, his defiance. He thought he'd earned this attitude because he was now a high school graduate.

"No, it's not over. Will you please get dressed again . . . now . . . so we can take some pictures," she yelled.

On cue, Dad stepped through the door. I noted how his entrance gave the scene a celebratory air.

"Well, hi there, graduate," he said.

Tim chuckled. "Yeah, hey."

Mom and Dad were rarely in the same room at the same time, a carryover from their relationship on Carlisle. I don't think either of them planned it that way; it was just an old way that never died. Dad was here, but now where was Mom?

"C'mon, outside, everyone," Mom directed as she stood near the sliding door to the patio.

And there we were, all four of us together for Tim's high school graduation picture, steamy breezes gently blowing behind us as we stood in the backyard. Tim wasn't smiling, his tie wasn't tied, his jacket was crooked, and his shirt was wrinkled and askew. Dad wasn't smiling either. Instead, he stood at attention with his arms at his sides, chin down as if posing by himself. Mom was there, smiling because she knew this recording of history must reflect happy times. I think she was frustrated, if not sad, that the scene was less than perfect. We looked so mismatched, so angry, so not together. We hung in the air with no movement like the lifeless humidity that hugged us.

The rightness and the wrongness of this scene were evident. The rightness was in Tim's graduation, an end to his old life and a new beginning with the freedom to be whomever and whatever he wanted to be. The wrongness was in the "should haves." We should have been happy as a family, celebrating this milestone with more family and friends. But we weren't, and we didn't. All we had was a telltale photograph.

Tim moved out of the townhouse on a summer day after graduation. Mom sat still in the dimly lit family room watching Tim carry small, encapsulated bits of his life across the room and out to his car in the garage. He took his home with him, remnants of the last eighteen years dropped into four small cardboard boxes. He plopped his clothes on the front seat and slid his possessions on the back seat, managing his keepsakes as if they were all he had, his only source of home. Tim was on a mission, and with only small talk among us and no time to waste, he breezed through the family room dressed in running shorts and a sleeveless T-shirt, wearing his sense of humor with a baseball cap plunked backward on his head. With a sense of urgency in his step, he looked glad to be leaving, to load the car, to drive off, to run away. He wanted out of a place that held him hostage with bad memories. I was happy for Tim because he was moving on, not out. He was starting in a new place, maybe one he could call his own home. Mom's response, as she surrendered to his departure, was silence. She understood that no words or expressed emotion would keep him from leaving.

We were moving forward in our own coping ways. Tim fled to a new house with new things. Mom's fear, anxiety, and general agitation with me and anything new became a cycle that had its phases to be worked through. And I tried to find correlations between my old and new homes, my old bedroom and backyard with my new bedroom and the confined patch of yard that was the patio. Oddly, I didn't miss Tim not being at home. Maybe I had become so accustomed to everything that was leaving me—my birch tree, my home, my father, my familiar—that Tim's absence did not affect me. He found a job as his own boss, working alone and managing a small distribution office. I think he liked it that way, as I, too, had once found contentment in being alone. He was establishing his comfortable familiar. He was eighteen, and I believed he would be okay.

I would see Tim that following year when he picked me up (I didn't have my driver's license yet) once or twice a month to meet Dad at McDonald's for dinner. Again, one of Dad's timely announcements fell at dinnertime. We ate our Big Macs, declaring that school was fine for me and work was fine for Tim, and everything in between was fine. Dad then announced he was getting married to the woman he had moved in with after he'd moved out of our home. Her name was Laurie. I realized his announcement was the true purpose of him getting together with Tim and me.

My burger and fries hit my gut with a *thunk*, rendering me shaky and speechless. Here was my father, who was no longer with my mother but with someone else? I posed this as a question, not a statement. I didn't know this man who had moved on with ease, and I questioned why he'd even bothered to tell us. I guess he thought it was the right thing to do. Bothering to do the right thing now seemed ironic.

Tim and I didn't have to say anything as Dad commented, "But please call me any time you need to talk." I found that to be a funny statement—calling him just to talk. Since we'd never talked when we lived under the same roof, I couldn't imagine picking up the phone to have a conversation.

Well, we met our obligation anyway. During the car ride back, Tim and I didn't feel the need to talk about Dad's announcement. We shook our heads in resignation that we had nothing to add. Our laughter was the conversation in which we found humor and camaraderie in an otherwise alienating pronouncement.

Soon Tim and I were invited for dinner to meet Laurie before their wedding. We arrived at their condo, which sat along the eleventh hole of a private country club. We expected no less of our father and observed what a nice situation he'd happened to fall into. Before pressing the doorbell button, we paused at the door to look at each other in understanding that we would lean on each other during this uncomfortable evening.

The bell's ring ushered our deep breaths. The door opened.

"Hi," Tim and I said in unison.

"Well, hello to the both of you, so glad you could come," Laurie said in her English accent. We noted how it was Laurie who greeted us first, and Dad who was slow to follow. She hugged us while planting air kisses on our cheeks. Her thin, platinum blonde hair tightly pulled back in a bun showed off her high forehead. Red lipstick accentuated her full lips, making her porcelain skin glow and her blue eyes clear.

"Hello," Dad said. "How are you?"

Dad invoked his clear, succinct voice as if to make an impression about living in a well-adorned condo with his lovely lady. Perhaps he thought he needed to make a pitch to us, as if we were skeptical clients.

"Good. We're good."

"And how's school coming along?" Dad asked.

"Let's sit," Laurie said.

As Tim and I surveyed the living room, I didn't know where I was. We spotted Laurie's things: fancy clocks, gold and glass tables, sofa and chairs in soft blue and cream. Dad's new place had none of the components of what I considered a home. He had none of his own things. I guess he didn't need the old familiar of home to establish a new one. His home was with his new partner. I was resentful with envy. I wanted to be like him, to feel at home even though I had none of my familiar and the rooms that defined it.

I don't remember what we talked about as we gathered in strategic places—Tim and I plopped together on the couch, and Dad and Laurie sat in petite stuffed chairs on opposite sides of us. I do remember we all nodded heads while replying "really?" and "just fine."

Soon Laurie was puttering in the kitchen, talking loudly to overcome dinner-prep noise and keeping the conversation going. Dad didn't say anything but felt summoned to the kitchen. I looked at Tim, and he at me. We smiled at each other and a chuckle followed Dad's rapid exit. We were thinking the same thing: *Where are we? What are we doing here?*

"Okay, I think we're ready. Dinner, everyone," Laurie said. Dad helped to carry the salad plates to the table.

"Lovely. This is so splendid that the both of you could come for dinner," she said.

I poked my salad greens. The carrot shavings were . . . shavings. They were the shavings of carrot skin with dirt speckles and hair-thin roots attached, nestled on top of the curls of the dainty lettuce leaves. Maybe it was a European thing? I found the dichotomy between this rustic presentation and her polished elegance amusing.

I could see why Dad was impressed with this woman. She had the aura of class, perhaps wealth, as measured by her surroundings, her accented conversation, and her red lipstick. Dad was showing us how happy he was in his new life with someone else. He was clearly divorced from what had been, including Tim and me.

Tim and I attended Dad's summer wedding. Though my brother and I had neither the interest nor the desire to attend, we assumed that we were going. I don't even remember Dad asking us. I think Mother was insulted when she found out Laurie was going to pick out the dress I was to wear at her wedding. "You let *her* pick out your dress?" she demanded, as if I couldn't pick one out myself with the help of my mother. I was stuck between justifying myself to my mother and pleasing the bride-to-be.

At their wedding reception in Chicago, Tim and I did not purposely remain distant from Dad but stood across the room because we weren't included in the social mingling. The only attention Tim and I received was from strangers at a distance. When we'd glance over at Dad, we'd see him pointing at us as if we were to be seen but not heard. He was acting out a connection with a nod of his head and a finger pointed in my direction, but really there was no connection. I was struck by the distance between us, even though he was just across the room, as Tim and I stood idle and alone. I overheard a conversation between a couple who appeared to be friends of theirs. The man remarked on how they had been together for so long. The woman completed the thought, ". . . and were finally able to marry." I understood their relationship had gone on for several years, while he was still married to Mom, while he still lived with us. This explained his frequent, lengthy absences under the guise of work.

At the time I was on autopilot, flying from one troubling scenario to another—how I didn't want to move, how difficult it was to make friends, and how alone I felt at high school. I failed to speak up and give a voice to my feelings. I thought the idea fruitless anyway because it wasn't about me; it was about my dad and his new wife, Mom working, and all the attention and help she needed. Tim and I attended Dad's wedding, whether we wanted to or not. "You should go. What would people think?" Mom said. I didn't let my voice speak through my action by not attending.

I had started my freshman year already in a deficit, with insufficient confidence from the remnants of divorce and losing the only place I had called home. I couldn't bond with the new house and school. They were too recent and unfamiliar. The commute to school and the loneliness of my days made it difficult to withstand even a single school day.

"Mom, I'm just trying to make it through each day. It's different at school, there's lots of work, and new people, and the girls are different. They're really smart. It's easy for them . . ." I tried to explain this to Mom as she prepared dinner in the kitchen. I wanted her to stop, put the knife down, and turn around to look at me. I hoped she would see the brink of my tears or hear the sadness in my voice or even feel my weariness as much as her own. How much I wanted my mom to sit with me a while and hold my hand and tell me everything would be all right. I needed a support and cheerleader like I had been to her when she was faced with something new. She owed me this comfort in kind. But she continued working in the kitchen, back and forth with her back turned to me, void of response.

Martha, my friend from Carlisle, was also my classmate, but her acceleration in classes, her membership in student council, and her other extracurricular activities separated us. We were no longer practicing friends but just two girls who had grown up together. What had bound us in girlhood had been detached. We had disconnected, my friend excelling while I moved laterally, trying to find my way with little progress.

I yearned for home, for the once-innate connections that I had embraced freely and automatically as Dad seemed to have done in his new home. Dad had started over, making new connections to a wife, friends, church, and home. He had done this with ease, as if the other end of the connection was already there, and he just had to join his end. I still struggled to connect with other ends. All I could see was that which wasn't connected.

if only I weren't fifteen

I turned fifteen the summer after I completed my freshman year. My journal writing started then with a pink hardcover book that invited me to fill its empty lined pages. A latch glued to the back of the book fit snugly into a lock glued to the top. I held my first journal in my hands, a gift from my mother. She thought every girl my age should keep a diary, especially a pink one. I thought so too. When I had been introduced to my new best friend, I had giggled, knowing I would soon be sharing my secrets. And then I grew serious. I was ready to transfer my thoughts and dreams and hopes from my heart, to commit them permanently to paper, filling my book with the joys of expectations. Neither out of reach nor out of mind, my journal rested on the middle shelf in the middle cubby atop my bedroom desk as the center of attention, where Nancy Drew mysteries, a black ceramic bank that was indeed a pig, and a small terrarium surrounded it. I lifted my book of secrets and confessions from its place, held it firmly in anticipation of forthcoming dialogue, and carried it to a sequestered spot on the floor at the foot of my bed, ready to commence writing upon release of the latch.

I began the first line of my journal entry: "I guess I got into the habit of writing my thoughts when we had to keep a journal for Morality class. . . . My mind has expanded so much so that I find a need to write things down." Journal writing fulfilled my need to organize my thoughts, to have a conversation with . . . someone, to feel not alone, to learn about myself. I was a young girl growing up, eager for clarity in an adult world I found disorienting. My vision of the world was not just about me but about everything else alive. I began to think about having a place, and that there must be a purpose. I yearned for inner guidance to navigate my world, to understand that there are other Nancys and houses and Carlisle Streets worlds away. And then I continued about some guys named Tom and Bob who were at my house with Lynn and Adam and what a great time we had.

My journal became the emotional cauldron of my yearning to meet boys—not necessarily to have a boyfriend, but to attract male companionship. That summer was great . . . well, good . . . but maybe not so good, because being fifteen was awkward with harbored yearning for male attention and social interaction with others my age.

I remember Bob, a stocky lifeguard with light brown hair and blue eyes, who worked that summer at the swimming pool next to the parking lot. I would watch him from my bedroom window as he sauntered, displaying any new athletic injuries to his legs with a stiffness in his gait. He was a college guy at Michigan State, and I was excited to have met a new friend. I wanted him to like me; I craved the attention and validation that someone wanted to be with me. It had been a long time since I'd felt good about something.

Going to the pool before dinner and on weekend afternoons was an alternative to staying home with my mother and having to share in her malaise, complaints, and sadness. I rested on my beach towel, draped on top of a sticky, strappy white plastic chaise lounge chair poolside, with noises on every level unconditionally welcoming my presence. This was my place to be at that moment.

It was weeks into the summer before I had enough confidence to say hello to Bob. Until then, the dialogue in my head played, rewinding to rehearse what I was going to say.

"I had to get in here, getting hot. Water is nice and cool," I said to Bob, squinting at him as he walked near the pool's edge. The sun and his face competed against each other for my eyes' focus.

"Yep," he said in a deep voice. I caught him stealing a glance at me.

"Busy today?"

"No, not too bad, except for these kids, lots of kids," he said, surveying the pool's dimensions.

"Yep."

"How long are you stayin'?"

"I don't know, till dinner or so. Why?"

"You comin' back after dinner?"

"I don't know, why?"

"Then it'll clear out and I can talk." He spoke as if our conversation were covert, with subtle lip movement and eyes concealed by sunglasses.

I was confused. I was excited. I was confident. I was feeling attractive in my own tanned skin wearing a bikini. With my womanhood underway starting in junior high, I wasn't toting my chubbiness anymore as I had through middle school. My maturity had worked with me as I entered high school; my petite frame was coming into focus.

Most nights I returned to the pool after dinner and stayed till closing. Bob and I would stretch out on our lounge chairs underneath a spotlight. The white cement beneath our feet glowed in the dark after absorbing the sun's rays all day. He and I were alone. The quiet was magical, the darkness mystical. Silence was punctuated by the rhythmic overtures of chirping crickets, buzzing cicadas, and burping frogs in a symphony that was so summer. The season slowed; I dreaded the ending of moments like these. The unity of Bob, me, and the summer's night created a dance where I swayed with the rhythm of present moments. Life was good again.

As the summer spent her days, I didn't know what to make of my friendship with Bob. As much as I wanted to encourage a special friendship, I couldn't. I got stuck. And being fifteen was the hurdle. I could not have made Bob more aware I was available to be a steady girlfriend or a Friday-night date. I would arrive early before he opened and stay late to help him close.

One morning the pool opening was delayed. "Come on, come with me. This rain should pass soon," he said, directing me to come with him to the clubhouse.

My heart raced. *Alone? With Bob?* I played it cool and met every step with his as he opened the door for me.

Inside I noticed the earthy colors of the room and the scent of damp, fresh wood as if I were in a cabin in the woods, only this house was in a parking lot. The chunky furniture, in shades from chocolate brown to light tan, was cozily arranged with a dark green carpet underfoot. The setting was conducive to an intimacy that made me uncomfortable.

I was cold and shaky sitting at the card table across from him. Maybe it was nerves, excitement, or the cold blasts from an out-of-whack air conditioner that contributed to my trembling.

"So, when do you think you'll reopen?" I asked. I tried to spark conversation, maybe initiating direct eye contact.

"Huh?" He raised his head from the sports page of the newspaper. "Probably in a couple of hours." He resumed reading.

"And you'll just stay here?"

"Yep, too far to go home and then come back." He turned the page.

I looked away from him to chairs in front of a large stone fireplace complementing the cozy structure, trying to pull something to say from the blank air space.

"You know, there's just not many people around here to be friends with . . . I just hate being fifteen." I thought I'd encourage personal conversation by divulging what was on my mind, as if bearing a secret to a clandestine lover.

"Why? It's okay. Nothing wrong with it. We talk. We're friends," he said. The sports page was clearly more interesting than I was.

"Yeah, I guess. Well, I'm gonna go now. I'll see you later."

Time had stopped for those few minutes. The intermittent pauses of conversation had shown me a lack of the connection I was hoping for, but I didn't care. All that mattered to me was being alone with Bob.

Labor Day 1977. My journal read: "As I look at the summer of '77, it was probably the best summer I have ever had. I met Bob, had great times with him, and I got the greatest tan. I think for the first time in my life, I kind of feel different in some way. Since all of the difficulties passed with the house and my parents, I now have time to think about me, where I'm going and what I'm going to do. I feel good about it."

I read that passage forty years later, and I see how I had started to direct my own destiny. I had started to pull away from the need for Mom to hold my hand, instilling comfort while ensuring me everything would be okay, to becoming more centered on what was making me happy. I was considering my wellbeing, taking control of life's offerings rather than the previous drama taking control of me. I was growing up.

No, Bob and I never dated or spent any time together away from the pool, but he did talk to me when he could. Brief conversations between us gave me hope that we were friends, even if he only asked what book I was reading. His conversation and acknowledgment were simple gestures I referred to as "great times."

The end of August came quickly, and his summer job ended. He was going back to college. I stayed with him till the closing of the pool.

"My last night here. Thanks for visiting during the day and keeping me company till close at night," he said as he crammed his backpack with sundries and headed to the pool's gate. He had never been this honest or personal with me before.

"So, can we stay in touch?" I asked as I followed his lead.

"Sure."

"Will you write back?"

"Sure. I may even call, easier for me."

I wanted to keep the conversation going and delay his departure, but I couldn't think of anything to talk about that would require his attention. I knew the effort would be futile, so I settled for a stroll next to him, noticing his hands' grasp on a textbook, notebook, and towel. Our arms swayed in sync with our tandem steps. I looked at him and studied his white teeth, blue eyes popping out of a tan face, and messy sandy hair. Would he hug me right now if I weren't fifteen? Would he kiss me? Would he tell me he'd had a good summer job because I was his companion at night when the pool was empty?

"I'll see you. Take care now."

I watched him sitting behind the wheel of his pea-green Vega as I had many times before when he'd arrive at the pool and park against the chain-link fence. I felt abandoned as I watched him pull out and away. He wasn't coming back. I stared unrelenting until his car disappeared around the street's bend.

I replayed our closing conversation, keeping my eyes shut to will his face back into my head. I didn't want to forget what he looked like, or a single word of our goodbye dialogue. He was going to write back, maybe even call. He gave me something to look forward to as I walked across the parking lot to the house. I replayed this assertion in my head to calm the surfacing doubt in my gut. During the school year, I wrote him a few times as if he were my best friend, narrating the minutiae of my high school life. I held on to the possibility that maybe he'd call just in time for the big spring dance. Would he go with me if I asked him?

"Sorry I'm calling kinda late . . . by the way, thanks for the cookies . . . they were a big hit around here . . . the reason I was calling was to tell you I got pinned."

"Pinned? Oh, wow, that's great. That's really good." *It all makes sense that he would have a steady girlfriend by now—and now he's calling to share the "good news" with his little-sister friend. To think that maybe he would have gone out with me if I just weren't fifteen. I hate being fifteen!*

My heart splintered with loneliness. I yearned for the attention, the familiarity of the connections I had left behind and was struggling to find again. Someone had stepped in to provide the feeling of comfort I got from knowing I was at home. He had made me feel at home.

elle

Driver's education class my sophomore year was a long-awaited event. I maneuvered my way into the driver's seat of a tan 1977 Ford Pinto. The days were warm that first semester in September, and the four of us, including the instructor, were tightly squashed in the two-door. I was stimulated and feeling adventurous. With warm wind blasting through half-opened windows, my cheeks flushed in response to the lack of air conditioning as the Pinto grabbed the open road ahead. I was steering. I was in control of something.

"Are we going on the expressway today?" I asked my instructor as I buckled up for safety in the driver's seat.

"No, nope, not yet," Mr. Johnson answered, talking to his clipboard while adjusting himself in the passenger seat. "We've got to learn to park first," he mumbled.

My question to him was an underlying metaphor for permission to break loose. I wanted to hit the road, to gas it past forty miles per hour to catch up to others. My need to overcome my awkwardness, feeling stuck and dull, translated to a need for speed. But first I had to learn how to maneuver through a situation in front of me, to learn how to park before I was ready to break for the open road. This sounded like a mandate for getting through the school year.

Getting up in the morning for school, especially during the winter, was always a struggle, not because I wasn't a morning person but because I faced an aura of anxiety created by my mother that spread like a virus due to her lack of feeling in control.

My only way to get to school was for Mom to drop me off at Martha's, who remained in the house up the street from the Carlisle house. Whenever we approached her home, I was reminded I didn't live on this street anymore. There had been many changes, yet this familiarity remained unchanged. I noted how time never erased the familiar, no matter how many changes affected me. My connection to this place was reiterated. My connection was timeless.

"No snow day. You've got school," Mom said one early winter morning. She turned, plunked a bowl of oatmeal down on the table in front of me, and clicked off the radio to which I'd been listening, hoping to hear the name of my high school.

"We'll have to take a cab to Martha's," Mom said. On many a snowy winter morning, she deferred to a surrogate driver.

"What? But it's just snowing now, there's nothing sticking on the ground. Can't you drive me yourself?"

"I can't drive in this. Please, Nancy, don't do this to me. Not now."

"Do *this* to you? What is *this?* What about me? It's always about you. Why can't you just drive like a normal person?"

My words cried out for her to take care of everything, seamlessly and without anxiety.

Of course, these arguments were too much for Mom and never ended in my favor. The arduous cab ride to Martha's made Mom and me edgy. When we finally arrived, Martha wasn't quite ready, so she politely invited us to step inside. Mom and I sat quietly in the family room until the calming silence lost.

"Martha, do you think I could bother you for an ashtray?" Mom whispered with a giggle. She was cajoling as if she knew she wasn't supposed to have one, let alone ask for it.

"What?" I whispered. "Can't you just sit without having to light up? You can't start smoking in their house. You'll stink it up."

I was mortified. I shot Mom an embarrassed look. There were no ashtrays in the house, but a decorative something was found. Mom lit up, took two puffs, and filled the clean air with plumes of smoke, enjoying her fix.

"I think we need to go, Martha," I said. I was being parental, taking control by extricating an offender. Martha's mom never did quite make it to the family room for the visit. Perhaps wafts of Nina Ricci mingled with cigarette odor had wound their way through the house, signaling to her that Mrs. Chadwick was present.

I started to realize during this school year that I had a voice to my feelings, and owning a voice meant I was gaining some control. Something as simple as learning how to drive became a metaphor for getting behind the wheel of my burgeoning adult life, in control of my steering while directing my speed and direction. I had spoken up to my mother about getting in the car and driving on those winter mornings and about her offensive smoking.

I was earning my grownup status. If-only-I-weren't-fifteen soon turned to sweet sixteen, where getting a license was an addition to my grownup ways.

My junior year of high school was just another year to get through. When it came time to visit prospective colleges, I dreaded it. I didn't know where I wanted to go or whom I should talk to. Pressure mounted to start planning now for something that was going to happen later—in two years—at a time when I was trying to live one day at a time.

It was difficult to focus on the future when I was still living in the present. As a young girl, my youthful innocence clung to me when I thought life could not have been any better, as I posed for my picture on my first day of kindergarten. My girlhood days were automatic, with each advancing school year temporarily interrupted by steamy summer days and warm, muggy nights. But after high school, I would be in a grownup world where adult responsibility would replace childhood ambitions. I prayed for divine intervention and guidance as I invoked my Catholic ways and the Lord. I tried to remain positive because I trusted it would work out.

I participated in college open house day in body but not in spirit. I wasn't ready to face that day of planning my future. I eyed the smiley people, representatives of popular private colleges, as I plodded past them, standing behind the brochures, placards, and posters displayed upon tables in front of them, resisting their grab for my attention to tell me they wanted me. But did I want them? How did I know now if I would want to be a part of them in a couple of years? I couldn't make these decisions. I was just trying to get through the school week.

"Hi, there," said Ms. Cella, my Morality teacher, from behind a table. "And where do you think you're going?"

"Excuse me?"

"Just kidding. No, umm, do you know where you want to go?"

"I have no idea." I shook my head. I couldn't say where I was going in the future when I didn't even know where I was presently. I had no sense of home or feeling rooted in school or on Pheasant Lane. I was overwhelmed, helpless, with no direction.

"Maybe Northern Illinois or downstate somewhere?" I replied, more as a question than a statement.

"How about Marquette? They're in Milwaukee. I went there. It's really a great school. I think—no, I know you'd like it."

After talking more about the school to Ms. Cella, I believed her. I was swept away by her excitement and looked forward to visiting this college.

My lack of direction had found a course. I had an idea of where to go, and I even had someone to talk to. But I faced another problem—my mother didn't drive beyond a ten-mile radius of Pheasant Lane, which meant no expressways and certainly no tollways. I'm not sure where Dad was. I don't remember him helping with my college decisions or planning.

I knew I would attend Marquette University even before I got there; it just felt right. I acknowledged the timing, alleviating my anxiety and hopelessness after a brief conversation with someone sitting behind a table. Optimism lifted my spirits, and I clung to hope to guide me forward.

I had prayed for answers to my questions and for direction to my aimless wandering, and I'd received both. But how quickly my college visit on a raw, windy, gray autumn day killed the spirit I'd been granted. Mom's best friend came to our aid as driver, support to Mom, and my savior.

"Finally, some lunch," Mom said. She breathed a deep sigh and plopped on her seat in the Student Union cafeteria.

"We've got a couple of stops to make afterward. We'll need to meet up with someone in the dorm who will walk us around," I said.

Mom stopped eating, dropped her ham sandwich on its wrapper, and looked at me.

"More walking?"

"Uh-huh."

"Oh."

I waited out Mom's pokey eating pace until we could continue our trek through campus.

"Oh, the wind. It's cold. Are we almost there?" Mom pleaded in halting words, trying to overcome the wind's strength as we struggled to walk up Wisconsin Avenue.

"We're on Twelfth Street. We need to go to Fifteenth."

"That far? Aren't there any buildings closer that we could see?" I was angry and disappointed. Why couldn't just one time, one day be about me? Why couldn't we enjoy this fall day, being excited—together? I wanted to make her see the positive things about the day, to make her realize that I hoped to be traipsing as a college student the very sidewalks we were navigating. I didn't bother to bicker, as I knew it would have been futile.

"Oh, why couldn't it have been a nicer day? It would have been more enjoyable to be touring when it's sunny out and not so windy and . . ." she said, struggling to keep up with my hurried pace.

"We're almost there," I said. "This will be our last stop, and then we can go home."

Our tour concluded late that afternoon, and I saw what

was necessary to make my decision. I replayed the campus tour in my head, walking that route again as a student in just two years. The car ride home was quiet; the silence was for different reasons. Mom's silence was because of her exhaustion; I was silent while imagining my new life.

ella

That summer would be my last summer to enjoy before leaving for college. I was content to sit at the pool, not alone but with myself.

Jim, a shy lifeguard, worked the evening shift. He was stocky and muscular with dark skin that tanned quickly and moppy brown hair lightened at the crown. We were young adults brought together in occasional poolside conversation because of our ages. He asked, "Are you doing anything tonight? I know this is kind of short notice, but I was wondering if you wanted to come with us—that would be me and Mike, you know, the one who works before me, and a couple of his friends and their girlfriends. I thought we'd all go to an outdoor movie or something. Maybe pack a cooler. What do you think? It *is* Friday."

"Sure, I think that would be fun."

An uh-oh thought popped, making me think twice about what I had said.

The problem I faced wasn't my hesitancy about going in a car with someone I hardly knew; it was telling my mother.

"You're what?" she screamed while standing in my bedroom doorway watching me change clothes.

"I'm going out tonight with Jim and some of his friends. Jim, he's the lifeguard across the street."

"No you're not. It's too late. You can't. You don't know any of these boys. You're going in a stranger's car. You could get stuck, in trouble, and then you wouldn't be able to get home."

I walked past Mom and out of the bedroom. "I'm going out, Mom. I'm old enough, and nothing is going to happen."

I tried to shake the uneasiness and lack of confidence that she had just instilled like osmosis. Could I be feeling this way because she'd told me to? Frightened? Uneasy?

The outdoor movie venue was dark with the screen's reflection of light bouncing off car roofs. Jim pulled into an available spot at the end of a row.

I didn't know what to do as we sat parked. The darkness drew out the silence among us. *Maybe I'll just sit here while we're all in here kind of tight?* I sat until someone gave me direction.

"I'm gonna get the cooler out," Jim said, getting out of the brown Mustang and heading to the trunk.

I was nervous. I anticipated the pressure to submit, to conform when the cooler's lid was opened. I'd never had even a sip of beer before, and wasn't sure I wanted to start then. My distraction by possible altered states of coherency made me unable to follow the conversation of the other passengers. I calculated in my head how long we'd been there, how long the movie was going to run, and then how long it would take to drive us home. It was going to be a long night. I was feeling stuck with no escape, should I need one, you know, just like Mom had said. But no one liked the movie. Jim drove us home. I walked in the door at 11:00 p.m. My fears were dismissed, but not without considering what Mom had said to me before I left.

That night I was startled to realize I was eighteen years old, ready to go to college, and uncomfortable with meeting new people my age. I had never been out just doing what friends do on Friday nights. I tried to dismiss my social ineptness by looking at the evening as a trial run, an example of a similar social encounter I was bound to have in college. I wanted to make friends, and this was an opportunity. I was also realizing my mother's words were in discord with the inner harmony I was trying to establish when meeting new people.

I turned to thoughts of conviction, to discover more of myself through connecting to others and, in turn, to my home.

My beloved part of my day remained five o'clock in the evening when the pool and sun deck had cleared. The chlorinated water calmed to intermittent ripples and bloomed teal as the sun lowered. I smelled the sweetness of summer when the calm winds sneaked through the open fields to greet me as I lay spread-eagle on the lounge chair. My world was heavy with the scent of wildflowers and freshly cut grass, with an added dried thorny-brush smell. Hints of chlorine were picked up as the fragrance wafted over the pool, piquing my concentration as the sensory bloom floated over me. I looked up as if I were being tapped on the shoulder. My serenity lasted for two hours. I didn't mind being alone while living in the moment. I could declare again, just as I had when that young girl posed for her picture, that life was truly good.

I realized home might not be limited in definition to a physical place. My first meaning of home was learned as a young girl when Carlisle, my birch tree, yellow walls, and all the physical remnants inside and out became the details to draw a picture as I had seen it once on blueprints. But it wasn't just being in a place. Friendships were also important to home.

I longed for a peace of heart and a settling of my spirit. Mom worked. Tim had his own place, and I didn't belong anywhere. The more I acknowledged my lack of belonging, the more alone I felt. It was as if I had big wad of gum stuck to the bottom of my shoe. I could peel it off, but there would always be a sticky residue that would never wear away.

But I would be off to college soon, and I wasn't going to let any end-of-summer rendezvous at the outdoor movie theater concern me enough to add to any social ineptness I already harbored. Perhaps if I let it go, ceased dwelling on what I lacked and how the deficits were holding me back, and tossed it all into the stratosphere to be blasted into tiny bits and disbursed into nothingness, I could be open to the start of a new life. I realized the past would be too heavy to carry to a bright new beginning. A renewed fervor inspired me to see that things weren't really that bad.

I struggled with what to say or do every time I saw Mom's face, which wore a defeated look that grew in sync with her sad demeanor. I tried to find ways to divert her unhappiness and loneliness to a different place. "Can't you find something to do, something to join where you could meet people? To get out and get involved in something?" I asked. She would chuckle, "I can't, oh, no," as if I were the silly one. This negation was her mantra whenever she considered doing something for herself.I realized I could never satisfy her needs, no matter how uncomfortable or out of my control they were. I could no longer be the fixer of what went wrong, dissipate the negative cloud that clung to her, or free her from self-pity brought about by her woe-is-me attitude. I believed now was the time for me. My heart smiled with the joy of expectation. I had permission to put myself first and to no longer be responsible for my mother's happiness. I never thought of this as being selfish in a vindictive way, but rather as the best way for us. Moving away from home gave me hope and a reason to believe I was going to be fine.

I thought of my birch buddy and wondered after all these years not only if it was still standing but also how it was standing. *Was it ever held back? Did it decide one day that it was going to spread out and grow with the budding of new branches?* I hoped it had experienced growth spurts just as I had.

After the pool closed for the season, I walked to fill idle time ordinarily spent within the confines of a chain-link fence, among sights and sounds of clustered connections to home. I had been a good walker around the house on Carlisle and took up the practice again easily. Early in my trek, I spotted tennis courts, their green surfaces aglow from bright white lights atop tall poles spraying illumination outside the courts and onto the remaining backyards of the last townhouse unit. I followed the high beams' beckoning call. I had reached the end of the path and the construction complex of townhouses and greeted the beginning of wild, growing things—a prairie with trees and waist-high weeds and the smell of sweet wildflowers and damp rye grass. What a contrast between a two-story structure painted in muddy greens and browns and an open, airy field of light, to see breezes tickle wild growth of diverse heights and densities moving in tandem with the wind's direction. Illumination from the lights and the stars took the lead for me to follow and to discover. Silvery tree trunk skins reflected their positions in the field. Birch trees! I heard their leaves dancing together when the humid breeze kicked up and moved the wild growth from right to left. I had never ventured this far since living here. Discovering the patch of birches that filled a wild field made me smile. The light from above told me my connections to home were not limited to my immediate surroundings but extended overhead to high places and beyond. I just needed to look up to the heavens to see a message of memories sent from a once-secure place I had known as home. The site told me I was in a better place. I too, like my birch buddy, was adaptable, taking root in once-empty space. The birch trees weren't quite full grown, but they had a good start in a new place, and so did I.

part 3

branching out

the blue and gold

Grabbing the mail on a cold but sunny January day was a blind pull from the box that hung just outside the front door. The familiar blue-and-gold logo of Marquette University popped from the white envelope. *My acceptance letter is here. I just know it.* My doubts about my acceptance converged when I heard my mother's voice in my head chime in: *This may not happen, you know.* I stared at my packet with analytical angst.

The director of admissions at Marquette University got right to the point in my acceptance letter: "Test scores and other data you have sent to us . . . certain of these items were slightly below the average of most of the students who enter our College of Journalism . . . concerned about the number of college-prep courses attempted during the past two years. A number of students comparable have been successful." I yelled at the letter, *Don't compare me to others.*

I am a good student. I proved it with my grades! I looked past the words "below average," which normally would have deemed me a failure, to see what was important: I had been accepted, and that was all that mattered.

It was mid-August and time to prepare to move— again. This time, it was a bittersweet change: part of me was happy and optimistic because I was moving on and away, yet another part of me saw loss and separation that had mirrored my experiences from the Carlisle move. Once again, I was faced with making new connections, rallying them behind me in support of finding home.

While I packed, I reduced my valued possessions to a concentrated home. Designated piles, some coming with me, others staying, were mounded on the floor. In addition to hauling bulging suitcases with four seasons of clothes neatly compressed into my Diane von Furstenberg luggage collection, I lugged a trunk. I thought this rectangular box to be a tidy, temporary home for personal possessions. It was like a time capsule whose contents would always stay in their original condition, telling a story about their owner. Encapsulated time would be a reminder of the days when home wrapped herself around me in comfort and security. Carefully selected remnants of home were concentrated because, of all the pieces I could have collected, the ones in the box— two houseplants, my journal, and a desk lamp, to name a few—were my strongest. Living things, my best friend, and a light to shine on it all were to merge with my adulthood. They would be plugs to be joined to new connections. Upon a lift of the hinged cover, my home and all its contents would be released to settle in a new place. Would they fit in? Would I fit in? Prospects of everything new—home, studies, teachers, friends—obscured my doubts. Newness implied a starting over and a pass that it was okay to leave behind the only home I knew for a place where I would learn more about me and the person I was going to become.

On a warm day in late August, I headed to college.

Though Dad did not help me with my college search or preparation, he did deliver me to school. I simply needed transportation, and he was it. Dad drove, and Mom sat silently in the back seat of his Cadillac Coupe de Ville. He loaded the von Furstenbergs, trunk, record player, and speakers in the Caddy's roomy trunk. I didn't look back at what I was leaving but looked forward to the idea of traveling with my possessions contained in a trunk in the car's back seat as an exciting new adventure.

I had to endure my present state of living with every mile traveled and every tick of ninety minutes before I could get to the side of new connections. The car's air conditioning failed to alleviate the leaden air contributed by three heavy breathers filling an enclosure of family members in name only. We traveled silently as if our minds were hosting private thoughts. I was relieved to acknowledge any interruption to our mindfulness.

Mom asked, "Did you take enough winter clothes?"

"It's only Wisconsin. It's the same weather."

I acknowledged the emotions that played out on her face, but I elected to not have them affect me. I was no longer responsible for her happiness. I was on my own, focused on a new course. I felt the way Dad looked: attention straight ahead, mesmerized by the traveling speed. I stared out the window to photograph the scenes and store them in memory while my eyes followed the roadside.

Neither Mom nor Dad had seized the opportunity to talk to me about being responsible or studying hard and getting good grades—conversation I had expected, if not encouraged. There were no warnings about dating and being aware of boys or of drinking too much. There were no wishes to have the best times of my life. There were no proud words or feelings expressed or emotions displayed. I wasn't surprised to witness another playing out of silence where the lack of conversation was a missing connection among us, the loss of a last chance to see that I had grown up. I was disappointed that they did not take advantage of the chance, solidifying any remnants of connection.

We exited the highway, and after circling a few blocks, Dad managed to park the car in front of my all-female dorm.

"Hey, this is it," he announced. He sounded excited, probably not because we had arrived but because it was finally time to get busy.

"We're here," Mom mumbled.

I'm here—I'm actually here.

Warmth and comfort greeted me in the small, cozy lobby with its charm in old wood and worn furniture in rustic browns. Mom and Dad followed at my heels.

"And we're not the only ones," Dad declared.

Mom added, "Yeah, look at everyone arriving, all your dorm mates. Looks busy. You really want to do this?" *No, Mom, I want to go home and stay there and never come out.* I never knew how to answer Mom's questions like this, other than sarcastically.

My attention was diverted to an oversized map of the United States glued to a corkboard hanging on a brick wall. Colored pins stuck to the map showed the places where the new students were from. Color was dotted all over the States, and I was excited to meet people from these representative pin markers.

"I'm going to bring in everything and get in line for the elevators," Dad announced. Mom hung in the background watching the commotion only female freshman could make. She followed me like any good shadow, whether because of stress, anxiety, or the pending notion of leaving without her daughter and being in the car alone with her ex-husband. I wouldn't have to be bothered by this behavior any more or to keep tabs on her feelings or inquire about her disposition. I wouldn't have to handle parental duties when she yelled, "I can't," underscoring the negative tones directed at me instead of having a supportive discussion with her now-adult daughter.

My room was at the end of the hall.

"It's a big room, a corner, roomier than I expected. I bet if we move these two beds against the wall, maybe, and the desks on opposite sides of the windows over here, we'll have all this floor space," I said.

"Well, sounds like you'll be busy for a while. We'll let you get started. It's time anyway that we get going. You've got lots of unpacking and organizing to do and meeting your roommate," Dad announced.

I was taken aback by his premature announcement. *Couldn't they stay just a little while, to help me settle, maybe walk around the dorm and campus so I could be comforted a bit?* I wanted to share my new experience with my parents, but their prompt exit said they didn't see it that way.

"Yep, I guess it's time," Mom said. She hesitated. I think she might have wanted to stay a while, but she was at the mercy of her driver's wishes.

Dad stopped to read two names from a small cardboard square affixed to the door. "Another Nancy—and she's from Texas. That'll be interesting for the both of you come winter," he chuckled.

I looked across the hall at a freshman's room as we stood in the doorway. Her mom was unwrapping new bed linens and making the bed. She unrolled the comforter, gave it a fluff, and tossed it on the bed, spreading it flat with her hands to smooth the bumps. The throw pillows got plumped too. A home away from home was being constructed, right down to the details. I was envious of the attention and time that a mom spent with her new freshman, but I knew my parents were not like the others. They didn't have a relationship between themselves, and they didn't have much of one with Tim or me. The closeness of family members I witnessed from my dorm mate across the hall was not us.

I detached myself from a place that did not exist to enter a place that was real, in the present moment, where I saw my own place, my first apartment, really. I accompanied my parents to the front doors of the lobby, and then I hugged them goodbye.

"Enjoy yourself. You'll be plenty busy," Dad said.

"Give me a call when you get settled," Mom added.

"I will."

I had held hope, though, that their parting words would be personal, affirming. I had grown to be a good daughter of whom they were proud. Perhaps my expectations were too much, hoping for an admission, a mea culpa, a realization that maybe they hadn't been as present and nurturing as they should have been. I had held out until this breaking point when I was no longer a child of Tom and Arlene, but my own adult self of Nancy. But no more time was necessary to linger and chat when all I needed to remember was to enjoy myself and call Mom later.

My parents, in effect, were good teachers. Admittedly, I'd had struggles and challenges growing up, but I had learned to be content with myself and that being alone didn't necessarily mean being lonely. I had learned from a nonpresent father to put a value on being present and from my anxious, nervous mother to be calm, roll with whatever was to come my way, and accept what I couldn't control. I consciously wanted to be the antithesis of both of them.

Beginning college was a turning point in my life, as if I had skipped ahead in years, growing to maturity and self-reliance, yet intellectually I understood I still had to live the college years ahead of me.

I watched them walk together down the sidewalk to the car. *Just what will they say to each other, if anything at all?* Cars were pulling up to the curb, and parents and students were getting out and unloading their belongings. Parents and their daughters interacted with conversation and animation. I witnessed the love and affection they had for one another as hugs and kisses and helpful gestures abounded. I heard parents talk to their children in new tones of adult conversation. Fathers took charge, and mothers wrapped their arms around their adult babies. I saw a life I hadn't experienced, but I knew my feeling of being alone was temporary, because soon I would be busy with class schedules and meeting new people and having new places to go. There would be no time to think about something I'd never had.

I looked ahead as the tiny moving dots of my parents faded into the distance. I walked back into the dorm lobby with a smile on my face and tears in my eyes. I would make good decisions. I was empowered. I owned what was yet to come.

I walked to the map of the United States on the lobby wall and looked over my shoulder to see a couple of girls standing behind me.

"Wow, look at this. We're from all over," one girl announced.

"Yeah, and from Hawaii."

"Look, there's a lot from Wisconsin, not a surprise, Chicago, too, and look at the East Coast."

I turned to the girl next to me and asked, "Where are you from?"

"San Antonio," the dark-haired, dark-eyed girl said proudly.

"Would you be Nancy Jo?" I asked.

"Yeah, that's me," she said.

"Well, I'm the other Nancy, your roommate," I declared as I introduced myself. "Do you need some help with your stuff?"

"Yes, thanks, but I really don't have too much."

"You drove from Texas? My gosh, how long did it take you?"

"Too long. I thought we weren't going to make it. We got a flat tire, and I lost a piece of luggage."

I recognized weariness in my new roommate's eyes, an exhausted expression on her face, though I had never experienced such a grave situation. I knew I was lucky, arriving intact with all of my belongings accounted for, and how terribly unlucky my new friend was to have lost a piece from home.

My new roommate and I went to our room to connect in friendship. My new family slowly introduced themselves to me, just as I amassed the tiny colored dots on the map, only they weren't dots anymore; they were real and counted, and I was among them. I had left home to start a new life in color; I had been set free.

big arms

At unexpected times during the day, I'd lapse into a desire to hear a reassuring voice tell me I was doing well and everything was going to be okay. I needed my own personal cheerleader. Now I think back to when Mom was faced with having to get a job. It was a new situation for her, a new place and people. She, too, needed a supporter, a personal cheerleader. Her experience and emotions at that time mirrored mine as a college freshman. We stood together on this one.

With any expectation comes a dose of reality that requires adjustment to the expectation. I faced my required adjustment early my freshman year when I yearned to be part of a social circle and make friends quickly. I wanted to join too, but I was having a difficult time, feeling awkward and socially immature.

I had an opportunity to meet new people and I was optimistic for the chance. A fruitful activities week was scheduled for the freshmen's orientation. I went to a party at my freshman advisor's apartment, and when I got there I studied my surroundings to teach myself essentially how to be at a party. I witnessed how others mingled and met new people with ease, laughing and smiling. The camaraderie was evident as both sexes enjoyed each other and fed off each other's interactions. No, they weren't like me, or I, them. I was stuck. I couldn't move; my hands and my legs were stiff like wooden boards, and my breathing was shallow. My awkwardness silenced me, and I knew that standing near the door blocking intermittent gusts of wind when it opened and closed was not my purpose for the evening. But at least I had something to do; I mirrored what I saw. I smiled constantly and laughed at nothing. I put one foot in front of the other and stepped into a vociferous group who appeared to have always known each another. I started yelling too, raising my voice above Bruce Springsteen's coming from stereo speakers strategically placed in each corner of the front room.

"Hey, great turnout," I yelled reaching the ear of a frumpy, redheaded, sweaty guy.

"Thanks! Glad you're here. How's your orientation going?" he asked.

"Just great, very busy, the schedule . . . the stuff we need to do, it's all been helpful," I was challenged to maintain conversation above the competing noise because I don't have one of those voices you can hear in a crowd. The tone of my voice blends in with the rest of the sounds, so I change the pitch when shouting in return, hoping to be understood.

"Well, I gotta give some stress relief to the incoming freshmen. I'm one of the GDLs this week."

"Oh, you are? I didn't know." *Dumb mistake. I should have known.*

"It's okay. I'm having just as much fun as you are, even though I have to be a 'group discussion leader.'"

I'd done it. I'd joined the crowd. I was part of something, even though it was just a party that lasted a couple of hours. This was an accomplishment; I had learned to be just like the others, working toward being a part of the university family.

And this is where I was not like my mother. My courage to break out and assert myself separated me from her. The party was an opportunity, a positive, to show my openness to others in order for connections to find their way to me. And I didn't have to answer, "You really want to do this?" when Mom would ask.

I sought relief from the heat and humidity during that September from flung-open windows in my dorm room where I encouraged the compressed air to stir. Retreating to my room in the evening after dinner, I'd see the curtains waving in warm breezes in rhythm with the new air, forcing the stale breath out. I sat on my twin bed, one of two beds that sat perpendicular to the wall closest to the door. The dimness of low light from two desk lamps made the room look and feel cozy, casting a golden glow upon the wood trim. The room was defined by twos, with two closets and two desks, which resembled shrines displaying trinkets from home as well as functional items related to our major area of study. For me, my two houseplants from my bedroom at home were thriving, and I noted their progress whenever I would sit to study or to write because it gave me a benchmark that I, too, had grown since leaving home. Maybe this idea developed from the birch tree planted in the front yard of my old home. Though my plants were no birch tree, they filled my need to have a growing thing, a reminder of home, nearby.

Reference books stood predominately on my bookcase where Nancy, my roommate, had framed pictures of her family grouped on hers. I didn't have any pictures of whom I had left behind. I didn't do it on purpose; it just happened.

I believed I would always have that homey feeling from Carlisle because I could not have imagined anything different. Living in the moment was innate back then, like referring to my birch buddy every time I looked out the living or family room windows as a reminder of my buddy's protective nature. The thriving foliage provided a way of life for me that was as much a part of my home as the ground it was rooted in. The bunnies, included. And now I was learning how to live in new, present moments.

I wondered how my tree was doing. I envisioned it well-grown, spread out in its space with mature branches hanging in arc shapes from its trunk with little leaves rustling in the wind orchestrating a *whoosh*. I measured my growth against my tree's stature as I imagined it. I had come far. I hoped my tree was still there and it had come far too.

One evening in October, my dorm mates were leaving for O'Donohue's Pub, but I wanted to stay in my room to feel the warm breeze and to smell the stale, sour air of the stockyards nearby combined with the yeast from the hops from the breweries across town. They weren't distractions; they were inspirations. I recognized how the aromas, whether unappealing or pleasing, could be a connection to my new home in a new way. I think it was a tap on my shoulder from God telling me he was with me and that I was in the right place, and I was just fine. My cheerleader had spoken.

ellie

That first year, I fed off my fellow journalism students and their creativity, fun attitude, outgoing spirit, and intellect, to the point of intoxication. I spent my spare hours at the J-school, loitering around the basement where, among classrooms and other offices, the newspaper office and photojournalism lab kept me curious.

I walked into the newspaper office one afternoon during the paper's looming deadline and saw Chris busy at the typewriter. I usually would never see my friend around campus without a camera around his neck, a pencil behind his ear, and a reporter's notebook sticking out of his back pocket, and here was no exception. He busted my "seen and not heard" approach.

"Hey, Nanc, thinking of doing some writing for the paper?" he asked.

"Me? No, nope, don't think so."

I picked up and read some copy Chris was working on.

"This is good, Chris. You're really good. And this is why I'm not a newspaper person. You've got a feel for this; it comes naturally for you . . . and not for me."

"It's really not hard," he said, as he looked up at me, grinning.

It didn't matter if it was difficult or easy—what he didn't realize was that my focus was on advertising.

In the fall, the J-school picnics were held on the last Friday of the month. Students congregated outside the classroom to celebrate a long week with beers and cheers. This was an opportunity to meet with other journalism students, and it was also a chance to make new, likeminded friends.

"Hey, you're in that mass communications class, the one we're required to take?" Ellen said with a smile. "And that professor . . . he wears . . ."

"I know where you're going with this," I said laughing. "He seems to have just two pairs each of pants, button-down shirts, and sport jackets in rotation. Though he does mix it up with a different tie . . ."

"I'm reminded of what day of the week it is by . . ." She stumbled over her words in laughter.

"What he's wearing."

I remember how the sharing of our stories of difficulties with a class or being in one with a really good professor brought us together. We studied hard and never stopped asking questions, whether in a media law or theology class. I was enveloped by happy people in my journalism world who made me happy as well. I loved being with my new family and living in my new place. Connecting to new friends was exhilarating, and because of them, I had found more of myself, enlivened.

But my slate of life was inconsistently dotted with remnants of social lagging from my teen years. I was confused when I met boys because I didn't know if I should view them as friends or as potential love interests. I hadn't had any experiences with them in high school, except my crush on Bob, where we never did get past talking about the weather and swimming pool traffic; I simply didn't know any boys. The boys I started to meet at school became my big brothers, friendships I relished, but which later created unrest because maybe I wanted them to be more. I wanted my social experiences to catch up with others—to be just like them.

The Gym, a campus bar, was a regular hangout for undergrads, including me, on a Friday night, with occasional graduate students filling in the bar stools. Male dental students appeared to be checking out the young ones as their glances and stares revealed their identities.

"Hey, how are you?" a dark-haired guy with a wide smile said one night.

"Me? I'm good. Fine. How are you?" I asked. I stood stiffly with an elbow resting on a sticky narrow shelf.

"Good. I'm Jim; this is Dave. We call him the 'kid doctor.'" I noticed how they looked like twins, both dressed in button-down shirts, zip-up jackets, and slip-on shoes.

"Hey, I'm Nancy. I don't think I've seen you here . . . do you go here?"

"I'm in dental school here," Jim spoke up, "and Dave goes to GW in DC for med school."

"Oh, I see . . . okay. I'm sorry, I didn't mean to keep staring at you, but you just . . . you . . . don't look like the rest of us . . . I mean, you look older, more reserved, I mean . . . you know?"

It was awkward. I was awkward. I'd been inviting attention with my stares and when I was called on it, I didn't know what to do.

But it was Dave whom I was stuck on at first sight. We talked about undergraduate school and graduate studies with the conversation evolving to a two-way encounter between Dave and me.

The final-call bell rang.

"Well, I guess it's time. It's still kind of early. Let's get something to eat. How about Angelo's?" Jim asked. I was thrilled to be escorted to the campus pizza joint by two graduate students.

I sat opposite Jim and Dave at a sticky wood table. Their direct eye contact from across the table intimidated me.

"So, what are two graduate students really doing with a freshman undergrad at one in the morning eating pizza?" Dave asked.

"I don't know," Jim said. He looked at Dave. "We're just out having a good time and found someone special to spend it with."

I didn't know what I was doing there. I was a young, naive freshman with a sudden crush on a medical student who didn't even go to my school.

"So, why'd you pick journalism?" Dave asked.

"I wanted to go into advertising, and the courses I needed to take were in the College of Journalism."

"What about it do you like?"

"I like the creativity; I like to ask lots of questions . . ."

"I noticed. Well, I have a hunch you're going to do very well in your field," Dave said.

"How can you be so sure?" I asked.

"I can tell. I can see you in a suit, with high heels, swinging a briefcase, scooting down Madison Avenue," Dave said. His sparkly eyes and warm grin smiled at me. "New York?"

"No, not New York, Chicago. I think I'll stay in Chicago."

My correction was swift, as if New York was an alien place where I wanted no association. I was possessive of Chicago because it was my place, where I came from, my home. I defended its existence as if its reality and my being were in doubt.

We continued talking for another hour until the cold, shriveled pizza told us it was time to go. We headed for the door.

"Well, it's been fun. Definitely an unexpected evening thanks to meeting a new friend. I'll see you, Dave, and I'll see you, Nancy, at the Gym again soon," Jim said, pointing to each of us.

Dave walked me to my dorm, stopping occasionally to turn an ordinarily fifteen-minute walk into an hour's stroll. We stopped in a dim corner away from the front door.

"You know, there are three very important women in my life named Nancy." Dave whispered. He stared into my eyes. I waited for him to tell me who they were, but he didn't, and I didn't ask. My question-driven nature was halted by the looks of an attractive, older man.

"It's been a great, fun evening, one I sure didn't expect to turn out this way," he said.

"I know. I'm sorry again for staring at you, I don't know what I was doing, it was just that . . . I . . . thought that you . . . anyway, thanks for the pizza and inviting me out and sitting and talking with me. I really enjoyed it."

"I've got your address and you have my mine. We'll write. I want to keep tabs on how your advertising studies are going. You're gonna do real well, Nancy. I enjoyed meeting you."

His arms held my body as they wrapped around my small frame. I buried my face in his soft shoulder; tears pooled in my lids. My arms encircled his torso and I held on for as long as I could. I lived the moments where a new experience of feeling connected to someone was a birth I had never experienced before. Another personal cheerleader offered assurance through his words and big surrounding arms.

"I'll see you soon. Maybe spring break I'll pay Jim a visit," he said. He walked away, waving, and I clung to the anticipation of seeing him again, for I considered it a sure thing.

A few weeks later as Dave headed into semester's end, he called me one Saturday night. Luckily, I'd stayed in to do homework.

"Hi, it's Dave."

"Hi, wow, you're up late. How are you? It's so good to hear from you, good to hear your voice," I said.

"I'm studying. Got a big exam tomorrow, and I'm just taking a break and thinking of you." I imagined him reclined on a carpeted living room floor in his apartment with his back against a comfy couch, binders and papers stacked in a semicircle in front of him—oh, while drinking a scotch and water, too.

"Where are you? At the library?" I said.

"No, I'm holed up in my room, at my desk that is too small for all that I need to read and review. So how are you? How's it going? How are all your studies?"

"Fine. Everything is going great. I'm managing to get it all in. I've got a good class load. I'm busy."

"You're getting out, though, too, aren't you? I mean, you're still going to the Gym?"

"I am but not too much, though. I enjoy staying in when it's quiet and everyone else is out."

". . . and picking up more grad students?"

"No, no way. What I've got is just fine for now." *Could I be any flirtier?*

"It is?"

"Yep. You're just fine."

"And you are too, Nancy. I enjoy your letters. You're beyond your years. You're really going to make it. I think about you. You are such a bright spot in the midst of my med school drama."

If only he could have seen the smile on my face and my eyes light up. I wanted him to know how much his personal words meant to me. I knew for sure that he was the best pen pal, best friend, best everything I could have wanted. At the beginning of every school term and the end, I hoped he would come to see Jim. But my hopes came and went as the school semesters evolved with each summer. "You are the kind of girl the guy falls in love with, the kind they marry and settle down with," he told me in a letter my sophomore year. *What's that supposed to mean? Does it matter if I fell in love with him that night I met him?*

I hoped we could sustain an exchange of phone calls, cards, letters, and visits, but his correspondence arrived sporadically, and the phone calls ceased. His words on one Christmas card during my third year were impersonal. I was a fool to think he'd stay in touch with me forever or return for a visit, noting our distance, studies, and his interest in another woman as certain explanations for his lack of interest in me. The reason he dropped me didn't matter, really, and when I realized this was only the start of many endings when I would become attached, I let it go.

I needed to move on and look forward, something I had drawn from my parents' divorce and the move from Carlisle. Time would allow me to see arms that surrounded me in welcome to my dorm life giving me stability and comfort. They surrounded me like a catalyst, sparking the discovery of a new family in my dorm, my college, and the entire university.

My young-girl self understood that my home was defined by the physical, the material possessions and places and rooms, but in my young adulthood I learned that people, a family of connections and community, were also home.

As my life experiences continued, I knew I wasn't alone, for a Jesuit university welcomed me into its home and gave me a sense of place, a renewed vigor for life, and a faithful rebirth in my belief in God. I was drawn to figuring out where I belonged and how I was going to fit in.

My understanding of the role of God in my life resumed after being dormant since eighth-grade graduation, which was probably not a good thing after being raised a Catholic, attending Catholic grade school, and receiving the sacraments. But attending a Jesuit university gave me an opportunity to reopen doors that had closed many years earlier and to look through them with both innocence and maturity. I was ready and open to have a new, different relationship, one I understood to be unconditional. My relationship with God became the only one that never caused anxiety, frustration, or loneliness for me. He was a connection I never questioned, doubted, or lost.

Gesu Church on Wisconsin Avenue was two blocks from my dorm and on the same block as Johnston Hall, my journalism school. I would pass those stately sculptured wooden doors and seek refuge there when I felt my sense of place losing its embrace, its connection with me. Stained glass circumnavigated inside walls that met the ceiling. I was drawn to these pictures and the stories they told. Every breath of musty, incense-laden air induced peace in my mind and heart. I heard the chants of religious leaders from many years ago, their rhythm echoing strength to the weak who faced them. I was surrounded with wonder peeking out from the church's beginnings in 1894. Whether I sat alone in a pew in the front of the church or stood in the back, I was in the presence of something. I wasn't alone; the air was filled with leftover conversations, deep meditations, and divine grace. And I was filled with a spirit where I believed God would always be with me and because of that, he would not let anything bad happen to me. He had big arms, too.

nancy undergrad

I walked into the law library for the first time as an apprehensive sophomore. I was afraid I'd be stopped because I was not a graduate student of law and was using the premises for undergraduate work. The law library was built in a circle with spacious floors, winding three floors tall. If you stood in the center of the library and looked up and turned around until you ended up where you started, you would have seen the entire law library. As I neared the front desk, I peered over the counter to see a law student slumped low in his seat. The light of the fluorescent bulb underneath the counter lit the top of his bowed head, which hung over his book. I dashed past him and was standing in the center of the library to assess where I might start when a gangly, dark-haired man with unevenly grown facial hair approached me.

"You need some help?" he asked.

"Umm, well, not really, but maybe you could tell me where I could start to find some information regarding the FTC and the NCCB?" I said. I stared at his full lips and white-toothed smile.

"The what and the who? Let me see that. What'd you have?"

I showed him my index card. "It's my journalism law paper I'm working on, and they suggested I start here. I'm hoping there's a case on it, and if this is too much, I can come back or just ask someone else. I don't mean to take your time away from . . ."

"No, it's okay, don't worry about it. I'm Alex, by the way," he said. I followed at his heels as he walked to the closet-sized room.

"I'm Nancy. I really appreciate this, really, a lot." Our eyes squinted at the florescent lights rebounding off the white walls and linoleum floor.

"This is Lexis. She's our wonderful friend who helps us with our case studies." He pointed to an oversized computer with printer. "Let's see what we can find." Alex grabbed a chair for me and pulled it next to his. "You caught me at a good time; I don't usually study here."

I wondered why he didn't. Maybe this was a place where only a select few students study—the real serious, brainy ones—and he wasn't one of them.

"This may take a few minutes depending on how much information there is out there. So, you're an undergraduate?" He leaned back in his chair, crossed his legs, and tugged at his scruffy beard.

"Yes, journalism."

"You do a lot of writing?" His black eyes narrowed. He seemed as curious about me as I was about him.

"Yes, I guess I do. But it's not just the writing. I'm kinda interested in the law and its relationship to advertising."

I wanted to get through this bump in my research and get on my way, but another law student popped his head in.

"How much longer, Alex?"

"Not too much longer. How's it going, Grover?"

"Oh, you know, same old crap," Grover said with a chuckle.

"Grover, this is Nancy, she's an undergraduate, doing a paper on a case for advertising and the law." Grover didn't look very law school–like with his short red hair and receding hairline, wire-rimmed glasses, and skinny frame. He was all legs and not much chest and torso, which made him look like he was wearing his pants under his armpits. He was cocky and quick-witted, and I thought that would make him one of tomorrow's best lawyers.

An uncomfortable run-in with my helper turned to embarrassment. I wanted to get out of there. I was pushing my luck with graduate students, as I was out of place because I'd stepped into a territory that was marked for others. My innocence and naïveté made me uncomfortable.

"Let me know when it's freed up, okay? Nice to meet you, Nancy," Grover said.

As he walked out, his eyes followed me as if to let me know I'd be seeing him again. He reminded me of a pesky schoolboy who never stopped talking to you.

"Well, let's see what we have," Alex interrupted. "Not too much. Do you know anything else about this case, so I can use some different key words?"

"Well, try the National Citizen's Committee for Broadcast . . . you know, it's a Friday night, and I'm sure you'd rather be in a more fun place than here," I said.

"Tell you what, let's finish this search, and if nothing comes up, come back and I'll help you further."

I was relieved. I didn't want to be a bother anymore.

"You want to go to the Ardmore for a beer . . . that is, if you aren't doing anything?" he asked.

"I'm not sure . . . I guess . . . you mean, right now?"

"Sure, let's do it," Alex smiled.

"I'll wait for you outside," I said.

I hurried out of the building to deeply inhale the night air as a sedative for my anxiety. I sat on the front step of the law library in anticipation of the evening. The unexpected always jumpstarted my analytical thinking, perhaps reading too much—that this was a date and he liked me more than just as a friend—where there was no story. Minutes later, Alex came up behind me and lightly touched my back, knocking me out of my future thoughts.

I thought all law students came from the same New England mold, like the graduate students in the movie *The Paper Chase*—sandy, curly-haired characters wearing crooked glasses that slipped down their noses. They'd be outfitted in button-down white or light blue oxford shirts with tails hanging out of their tan Chinos, maybe an off-center dark tie loosely hanging from their necks, too. They'd always carry notebooks and accordion file folders that slipped away from their grips as they hurried . . . somewhere. They looked like they just woke up and grabbed whatever was in sight because they were always late for class.

Alex was different. He didn't fit my character study because he dressed in loose-fitting worn jeans and an oversized, red casual shirt that hung over his slouching, skinny frame. He looked Italian, but I was promptly corrected. "No, Sicilian." He didn't appear to have the discipline and the seriousness of the other law students. Maybe it was just that he was really good at learning the law thing.

After a couple of beers and easy conversation at the nearest bar, we strolled to my dorm.

"This is me, rather convenient to the library," I said.

We slowed our pace.

"Yes, it is. So does that mean I'll be seeing more of you there?"

I kept looking past him, over his shoulder, anywhere but at his face. He was engaging with those black olive eyes, but I wasn't with my roaming green peepers.

"Well, maybe, because it looks like a great place to study."

"Good, and not many law students study there, so there should be room for you. Let's keep walking. Do you have to go in right now?" He took my arm.

As we started to walk, I saw groups of friends and couples walking, enjoying the warm evening, and I saw myself as one of them. The more we talked, the more I was at ease and no longer needed to question what he was doing with me. After stops and starts along Wells Street, Alex put his arms around me in a snug embrace. I was comforted as we stood close together, talking and laughing. I was glad to have made a new friend.

I continued to study at the law library that semester on Friday and Saturday nights when law students were usually not there. It was true that Alex didn't study there, because I never saw him there again. I was disappointed. Why didn't I hear from him after we had such a nice night and enjoyed each other? My mind told me to drop it, forget and move on, but my heart was sad because I wanted to see him again.

That following spring, Alex saw me walking away from campus.

"Hey, where you going?" he yelled, trying to catch up to me. I stopped and turned around.

"Hi. Going home for Spring Break. Taking the Greyhound." I continued walking. I wasn't interested in being picked up again.

"I'll walk with you. Here, give me that, I'll carry it." He grabbed my duffle bag and put his arm around me like an old friend as we continued to walk.

"C'mon, let's stop over here, at the park, he said."

Though I had nothing to say to him, I did have a few minutes to spare.

We sat on a hill blanketed in cool grass, overlooking the intersecting highways of exit and entrance ramps. A steady drone of traffic noise broke, occupying the silence between us. He acted as if he was picking up where we had left off that night after the library.

"Great day, isn't it? C'mon over here, get closer," he said. His face was about as close to mine as it could get. His stare drew me into him.

"When are you back?" he asked.

"Next Sunday."

"I'll call you then, later that afternoon. Maybe I'll come over, and then we can do something?"

Yeah, right. Alex stretched out on the grass, hands behind his head, legs crossed. I sat cross-legged, ready to stand and make a dash. Our attention was diverted to rustling sounds in the tree branches ahead, created by two squirrels performing gymnastics. The branches rustling in slight breezes changed my focus. I eyed the limbs, tracing them down to the tree's peeling trunk, and discovered a mature birch tree with long, overgrown branches that appeared connected.

He pointed to the tree. "What do you suppose they're doing?"

"Don't know. Looks like they're having fun," I said, laughing. "Why can't we do as the squirrels do?"

"We can."

"Uh-huh. I gotta get going. I need to buy a ticket."

He never called that Sunday afternoon. I missed him. No, I missed the feelings I'd had with him when we first met at the library, happy and excited. I was as eager to learn about someone new as I was about opening myself to being learned about. I'd wanted to believe he was interested enough to date me, but he wasn't, and we didn't. I had to see him exactly as he was: someone who helped me with my schoolwork, someone with whom I went out once and had a nice time.

My birch tree told me to loosen up and enjoy the playful opportunities. After I put this into context, I accepted what was and lived the moments as they were given to me. *They are there. Just look.* I became more accepting of what I could not change. My birch buddy told me home could also be a snapshot of time where the mix of person, place, or even a couple of scampering squirrels can give pleasure, laughter, and a smile. I carried a connection to the outdoors, starting in my youth with my birch tree and a bathroom window, to the smell of hops and the stockyards seeping through open windows in my college dorm room and the simplest connection with squirrels in a birch tree.

elle

I continued to study at the law library and to meet more law students, all men. I could count the number of female law students on one hand. I was drawn to making new connections with others, as I believed they were what I had lacked long ago.

"Hey, we didn't think you guys were coming," Mike said. He was leaning on one elbow at the bar in O'Donohue's Pub.

"Yeah, yeah, we're here," Lexi, my roommate, said.

"I see you putting in some hours at the law library." I found this statement to be a leading one, rather lawyerly.

"Huh? How do you know that? I never see you there."

"Oh, come on now, word gets around," Mike said.

"Those guys have loose lips. Aren't they supposed to be studying instead of watching who's coming and going?" Lexi said.

"Well, we all know you now. You're Nancy Undergrad," Mike said.

"Huh? I'm who?"

"We call you Nancy Undergrad, cause you know everyone and everyone knows you, kind of like a mascot."

Though it was an endearing term, I was embarrassed.

I had no business hanging out with grad students; I had overstayed my welcome. But I pretended to be blind and loved every minute of the attention. I became anxious when I wanted someone to like me in a way other than as a little sister. I looked at "Nancy Undergrad meets male law student" as a pairing where both sides benefited. The few friends I made were intoxicating and awarded me validation in exchange for stroking their egos, filling their empty places. I learned I could have male friends who were not boyfriends, but I remained an anomaly, an unexplained something they didn't know what to do with.

My graduate circle of friends expanded to include the dental school. Only this time, I had no interest in dentistry and did not even consider studying where the dental students studied. Lexi and I were regular dinner buddies in our dorm's cafeteria, where we'd find the dental students also eating.

"God, just look at that round table over there," Lexi said.

"They're always there, up close to the front."

"So they can see all the girls walking in for dinner," I said.

"Yep, that's it. They are the Knights of the Round Table," Lexi said loudly. She wanted them to overhear her words.

The Knights acted upon their belief that the women of the dorm were "fresh and young" and rather in need of male companionship. Lexi laughed at their assumptions only because it became them. Their egos and wild partying and thinking they were the dorm's gift always gave Lexi and me something to scream about. Conversations among us stirred provocation.

"Got to watch those pounds," John said with a chuckle.

"I don't have a problem with that," I said more loudly. The table of three erupted in laughter.

I was lucky. The "freshman fifteen" never invaded my body. In fact, I lost weight. Since I was on a prepaid meal plan, I had to eat cafeteria food. The broccoli was over-cooked to army green. I chewed pizza, tomato-flavored cardboard. I drank a lot of milk, had the salad bar for dinner, and topped my meals with vanilla ice cream for dessert. My circumnavigation of campus wiped out most of the calories I consumed.

One of the Knights, was a short Italian who Lexi nicknamed "exhale" because he looked like he needed to, with his beefed-up upper body and muscular arms that couldn't hang close to his torso. I wanted to know more about his quiet and reserved nature, so unlike his dinner companions, whose loud conversation and dramatic body language demonstrated otherwise.

"Hey, you guys, can I join you?" Diane, a third-floor RA asked. "What's so funny?"

"We were commenting about some of the scenery," I said, pointing to the round table.

"You know the Knights of the Round Table, Diane?" Lexi asked.

"I'm familiar with them," Diane said.

"You are? How . . . I mean, who . . . are they?" I asked.

"The dark, short one, he's got lot of friends but you never really see him with anyone. He's shy, quiet. He gets around, though."

"One-night stands?"

"You could say that," Diane said.

Our suspicion was confirmed one Saturday night when I saw him in O'Donohue's Pub. I purposely walked around the crowded, dark bar to meet him. He was alone, but maybe he wouldn't want to be leaving that way. Small talk progressed to honesty as he dampened my fantasy.

"I just can't," he said.

"What are you talking about?" I asked.

"No, no I can't." He gazed over the bar to the crowd on the other side.

"Huh? I don't think I've asked you for anything."

"No, you haven't, not really. Do you know why I'm here or what I'm doing?"

The conversation was odd, confusing, and abstract.

"No, haven't any idea. Maybe you are waiting for someone, and they haven't showed?"

The bar's volume increased as louder shouts from students ordering refills traveled from one side of the bar to the other. We stepped closer into each other as our conversation became serious.

"No, no, that's not it. You see, I can't take you with me tonight, home, with me."

Huh? I was shocked. I wanted to dash from embarrassment.

"I . . . I . . . but . . . I never asked . . . I mean, how about . . ."

"You are just too innocent and nice. I can't do that to you. I mean, I could, I could ask you to come home with me, and you would, and the next morning you'd expect something. But that would be it. I wouldn't be giving you what you want. And I can't do that to you."

"Okay, then, well. I'll be going. Have a nice night," I said as I plowed through the crowd to reach the front door and burst outside.

I heard a shout. "Nancy, wait up."

My embarrassment kept me walking.

"C'mon, I'll walk you back." He took my arm.

"You don't have to, really, you don't." I was getting angry. I was mad at . . . him? And why? I wasn't a girl to be picked up, and I was angry to think he thought I was available for just one night. My anger stemmed from my awkwardness that my interest in him was so obvious that he felt he needed to push back, a result of miscommunication. We stopped in a dark corner in the parking lot next to my dorm, leaning up against the building. He took my hands in his, stepped closer to me, and kissed me gently on the cheek.

"I'm sorry. That was bad what happened. I didn't mean it for you. You are so nice."

Okay, so I melted at his apology and subsequent compliment. I wasn't mad anymore. I let the whole thing go. We had cleared the confusing air.

I was on a slow track, experiencing in college feelings and emotions what most other women my age had already weathered through in high school. *It wasn't a bad thing. Right?*

When I returned to my dorm room, the dialogue in my head was replaying itself continuously. I couldn't find Lexi, but found Nancy, who was awake and willing to listen.

"Look at all the male friends you have now. You're always talking about the guys at the law school and now those dental students. You've said you're interested in a couple of guys in J-class. I'd say most women around here don't even know as many guys as you do," she said.

Her objective observation was correct. However, I tried to defend myself with a different spin.

"But that's just it. I don't go out with them. I'm a little sister to them. They want to slap me on the back and say, 'Here, have another beer.'"

"And most of those guys are in grad school."

"And I have a lot of fun with everyone in my J-classes, too. They're good and smart and are great to hang out with, but none of the guys look at me as someone to go out with."

My anxiety wasn't about boys and dating. It was the effect that boys and dating had on me. I felt bounced from one bumper to another in a never-ending game of pinball. I couldn't reconcile being happy, anxious and frustrated at the same time. Perhaps it was because I had immediate expectations. The highs and lows continued to circulate in my head. "I can't believe someone like you doesn't have a boyfriend," was a consistent comment by most of my male friends. The pressure to have a boyfriend was consuming me, and I didn't understand why "someone like me" couldn't get one. But I admitted that even if I were ever to be a girlfriend, anxiety and torment would still exist. It wasn't meant to be; I wasn't ready. My quest to increase my friendships and their connections was very complicated.

My birch tree gave me a focal point to refer to, a kind

of meditative bull's-eye to hit every time I stood in front of it in greeting, contemplation, or conversation. It kept me centered and reminded me that there would be times of difficult growth, but the sun would shine on me the next day, and I would be renewed in spirit.

I deferred to taking long walks, inviting my mind to wander and my heart to become peaceful. My personal field trips took me to downtown Milwaukee and over the bridge to the lakefront. The grassy canvas invited me closer, to touch the whitewashed boulders and see them lumped in stacks, to hear the waters rush and crash against the shore. The dimming sunset as it met the horizon and fell with a rhythm to the water's music comforted me. When I returned to my dorm room late in the afternoon, my journal witnessed the scrawls of constant ink flow, with adolescent-sounding confusion, pangs of frustration, and turmoil of love in motion, coloring a white space. The dialogue between my journal and me was honest and open, just like best friends. I wanted a best friend.

During my study nights at the law library, Grover usually made it a point to stop and talk with me. As if impressed with himself, he did the talking while I listened. At the end of the school year, he gave me a peach-colored rose and a note card for me with his full name imprinted on the top of the card. He apologized if any of his actions had offended me throughout the year. He said he'd found me "refreshing" and he'd enjoyed "being friendly" with me. That same year, another law student sent me a "Deepest Sympathy" card, a sarcastic take on "thanks for being friends." Nancy Undergrad was confused.

relationships

One Saturday night, Lexi and I made a lasagna dinner for three dental-student friends—more big brothers. Why we decided to make dinner for a bunch of dental students is beyond my understanding. I had no desire to be a dental-student groupie. I also didn't want to be looked at as a sister who was so fond of her brothers that she was willing to make a home-cooked meal for them. My attraction to Brad, a mix of curiosity and the need to know why he continued to stare at me in silence, was relentless. I didn't know what to make of my new speechless friend. Jeff was our neutral intermediary, an interpreter for confusing dialogue between grad student and undergrad, and an all-around good buddy.

Lex and I landed our plates in front of us on the table after serving the boys. After bites were consumed in silence, Jeff piped up.

"Hey, we still have time to catch *Apocalypse Now* at the Varsity. Let's go."

Lex and I looked at each other as if the evening had been fast-forwarded and we were still reading the opening credits. We yielded to the unanimous decision. Off we went.

While two of the boys walked ahead of Lexi and me, I looked over my shoulder to see Brad at my heels.

"He didn't say anything at dinner, just stared and nodded his head. Didn't you notice?" I whispered to Lexi.

"What's his problem? He's shy? He didn't want to be there?" she said. "It's starting to make me think he's just weird."

Brad ushered Lexi and me into the aisle, followed by the boys, with Brad on the end. Brad and I were bookends. I guess he didn't want to sit next to me.

Lex and I continued to take advantage of any opportunity we had when crossing paths with the dental students, which was usually on a Friday night in the usual campus bars. One bitter cold Friday night at the Gym was no exception.

"Hey, you know what?" Jeff said. "You two ladies really need to relax a little, you know, let loose."

"Huh? We couldn't be more relaxed. It's a Friday night," Lex said.

"Another beer would certainly help you," Jeff said.

"Jeff, you know I don't even like beer . . ." Lexi said.

"And one is my limit, I'm a lightweight. Okay, maybe two, but that's it," I said.

Lex and I turned away from Jeff to face the bar and see a pitcher of cold brew under our noses.

"Drink up, ladies," Jeff said. "It's for you."

A couple of Jeff's friends soon joined us, and Lex and I were relieved from our prescription for relaxation when the dental students grabbed the pitcher for their own consumption.

I was not much of a beer drinker. In fact, beer made me feel worse—sick, tired, and not wanting to be with others. I would start to feel loopy from staying up till 1:00 a.m., not from overindulging alcohol. I didn't need it to unwind or relax. Just being with friends loosened me up.

That winter evening, we closed the bar. Lex and I never finished that pitcher—it was done for us, I think. I had been ready to leave hours before; I was tired.

"It's time to go. See those lights blinking? Did you hear the bell, Jeff?" I yelled. "God, we've got a walk back, Lex. Let's get going."

"Hey, where you goin'?" Jeff asked.

"Back to the dorm," I answered.

"Hey, no, not yet, it's still early," Brad's roommate, Bart, yelled. "Come on over to our apartment. It's a lot closer than walking back. We'll put on some music, wind down, you know?"

Lexi and I looked at each other in mutual contemplation.

"Well, if we're going, let's go," I said.

Piercing high winds accompanied our walk. There was no turning back.

"What's the front desk going to say when we walk in early Sunday morning, looking like the night before?" I asked Lexi.

"We just got back from church," she replied as a statement and not a question.

When I walked into Brad's apartment, I anticipated a burst of heat but was not granted the relief. Even though I was bundled in a white turtleneck shirt, red wool sweater, and a short white quilted ski jacket, I was still shivering. The sparsely furnished apartment reflected a temporary stay and limited hours in residence. Scratched wood floors reflected the sliding of chairs and tables to fit their preferred positions.

To help us settle, we sang to the guitar strumming of Harry Chapin playing from the turntable. A well-worn and overstuffed fuzzy brown couch, a couple of chairs, a beat-up old coffee table, and stereo equipment sat haphazardly in the room. Lexi insisted the top of a threadbare rug would be a fine place for her to recline. Brad followed me after first inviting me to the couch.

"I'm okay, actually, just fine. I'm wedged in here good. You sure you got enough room?" I asked. "You can hold me, you know. It's okay."

I looked at Brad's face. *Yep, just staring at me with a smile.*

No one stirred until the wee hours of the morning, when Lexi and I slipped out unnoticed.

I thought how sleeping next to a guy could be so innocent, comforting, and familiar. Like home.

One Saturday, Jeff's friend Butch, Lex, and I were at Jeff's apartment listening to the Beatles' *White Album* while engaging in adolescent discussion.

"So, what's going on with Brad these days?" I asked.

"Brad? Oh, I guess he's been busy, haven't seen him much," Jeff replied.

"I see. I haven't either," I said. "I don't get it. We go out and see you guys every once in a while and have a really fun time. But I can't seem to be with just Brad, alone."

"It doesn't mean he doesn't like you and doesn't want to hang out with you. He just doesn't have the time," Butch chimed in. "Look, you guys are great, and you're a lot of fun. I've never really gotten to be friends with undergraduates before. Just relax. Don't push. Have a good time with undergraduate school. Let it happen, man." He bobbed his head and sang with Paul McCartney's "Rocky Raccoon": ". . . but everyone knew her as Nancy."

Lexi waved her hand with a laugh. "It's just all too weird."

Brad and I never dated. We finished the school term, and Lexi and I didn't see the guys again. I was still reminded of the feelings Brad had invoked in me and questioned how I could really like someone I didn't even know and why I was trying to make something of nothing.

I realized I already had what I'd been yearning for. I had a group of friends with whom I could talk about what was going on in my head, and they would listen. I recognized their patience and reassurance and was grateful for it. They did not dismiss me because I was an undergrad who was exhibiting a bad case of growing pains, but accepted that as just who I was. They taught me that true friendship is accepting people as they are and that the connections are unconditional.

ellee

I moved into the Belmont Apartments on campus for my junior year. The dark, drab concrete exterior matched the dinginess inside. I positioned my daybed along the longest wall to give me a view of the entrance to the main campus, brightening an inherent somberness. A table and pair of chairs sat in front of a picture window in my kitchen, adding to my dining pleasure. I did my own cooking and so did not have to partake in a meal plan at the dorm's cafeteria. A stuffed chair and ottoman, centered in front of a large window overlooking center campus, gave me the reflective space I often required at the end of the day after a full class load. An old metal desk was my television stand, and a small wrought iron plant stand served to hold my limited book collection. My independence and sense of place with my apartment as home, a microcosm within my larger home world, was important, giving me confidence and a way to discover more of who I was becoming. Dad would call maybe once a month; I never thought of reciprocating.

"Hiya. How's it going?" he'd always ask.

"Going okay. It's hard. So much studying. Lots to read, and there seems to always be a test."

"You got enough money?"

"Yep. Not a problem."

I remembered Mom's words to me: "He was always a good provider." I didn't think to chastise myself when I considered that Dad's provision was limited to money when it should have included emotional support and personal interest. It was just the way he was and continued to be. I remembered only talking to Mom as necessary.

"I was out last night and . . . I kind of . . . lost my wallet," I confessed to Mom on the phone one Saturday morning.

"You did *what?* Where were you?"

"I was at a bar, not far from here, and it was crowded with lots of pushing through to move around. I don't know how it happened. Don't worry, it's not like I had a lot of money in it. I'll check back there when they open later tonight."

"Oh . . . I stopped by to see your brother after my dental appointment."

Oh, God, stopped in on him unannounced? Why?

"Since he lived so close to the dentist and it was such a nice day. You know, he was out mowing the lawn? Your father could never get him to mow the lawn when . . ."

"Okay, Mom, okay. He was taking care of his place. I'm sure he's doing just fine with working and keeping house."

"I wasn't allowed inside, though."

"That's probably another good thing."

I don't remember Tim and me talking on the phone

during my college years, probably because Mom kept me up to date about his wellbeing and what he'd been up to. Seeing Tim and Mom on holidays was enough to keep us plugged in to each other.

And I did get my wallet back. O'Donohue's called and said they were holding it.

elle

In my third year, I realized not only how much I had grown up but also how far I still had to go. Getting to know these male friends last year had been a whirlwind in desire and anticipation with an overactive mind as the driving force. *Why doesn't anything work out? If I'm so great and cute and fun to be with, why don't I have a boyfriend?* I also wondered why I hadn't heard any of my female friends sharing similar sentiments. I reasoned they either had boyfriends, or they couldn't possibly be bothered with them and just didn't care. It was high school talk, and I didn't want to embarrass myself by bringing up the subject of boys when an eye-rolling reaction from the ladies was sure to follow. I chastised myself for thinking that the topic of males was the only conversation among women whose emotions were the key element in female bonding. I saw how my women friends were comfortable with themselves, seeking fun and overall enjoyment of their days.

"Lynn, Deb, and I are going to the Mug Rack on Friday for the concert," Carol, my former dorm mate, said to me. "You wanna come? They usually have really good bands, and the Union is never too crowded at that time."

"Let's do it. Anyone else going?" I asked. I was hinting to see if any guys were included or if we'd be meeting anyone knew.

"Don't know. I just had a really long week and want to rock out and get crazy."

I noted how Carol kept her focus on herself and did

not make mention of anything that had to do with boys, enjoying a Friday night with a few friends and letting Carol be Carol. I especially recognized my ease at joining the craziness, dancing, and laughing. I didn't need the subject of anything male to be what bound my female friendships.

My perspective of the male friendship had shifted. I had male teaching assistants—graduate students—for photojournalism and British literature, and had viewed the teacher–student relationship as bounded by a line until I got to know them, and that included outside the classroom.

"We're off to O'Donohue's, want to come?" Chris, the quintessential newspaper guy and my good buddy asked me at the end of class.

"Sure, sounds good."

"Tom and John from the paper are coming. Rick said he's coming too."

"Rick? Who's Rick?"

"Mr. Johnson."

"You call him Rick?"

"Yeah. We've hung out before. He's cool. We've had a couple of beers, shot some pool, you know."

"Really? Like you're good friends, huh?"

I quickly saw how a rapport could be developed where a friendship could be forged between student and teacher.

During a midterm exam in British Lit, we had to write an essay about a piece of literature that created laughter after a serious discussion in a previous class. When I finished my exam, I handed my blue book to Mr. Sullivan. He scanned it while I stood in front of him until he worked his way to the end page where he read, ". . . and that's all I can say about this because that's all I know because we started laughing and didn't finish discussing the analysis." Our laughter turned our faces red as we recalled that discussion. We walked out together.

"Thanks, Mr. Sullivan, for a great class."

"Thanks, and it's Denny. You can call me Denny up until I get my law degree. And then it's Mr. Sullivan."

Denny? He wanted me to call him by his first name?

I was learning more about how friendships can be deepened by watching a few female friends become more concerned with their happiness and wellbeing, and where the removal of a boundary line ignited new friendships outside the classroom. I had seen the role of laughter and not taking myself too seriously as friendship-maker.

ellæ

By the end of the school term, I was tired of my boyfriend-less angst, drama, and questioning why nothing works out for me. I reasoned I couldn't grow until I let go of that preoccupation. In releasing, I had made room for newness that had become integral to my adult life's outlook.

One day I was strolling through center campus and stopped in front of the St. Joan of Arc chapel, dating back to the early fifteenth century, brought from the village of Chasse in the Rhone Valley, southeast of Lyon, France. This intimate place was a haven for prayer and reflection as the heart of the university community. There was something about this reverent, small structure that offered connections, grounding, perhaps recentering, to me and to others who would stand in its presence. My mind captured snapshots of gratitude, replacing my outlook of what I didn't have with what I did have, acknowledging the growth of my many connections. I realized my belief in God was maturing too, and that my reliance on something unconditional would always be there for me. Classroom knowledge about God and evolution into a daily practice of a faith-driven life had become part of my membership in the Jesuit community. Perhaps it was both, maybe the same.

Marquette gave me not only a sense of place but also a sense of being, beyond the physical connections. My understanding of the role of God in my life had evolved from my first memory of praying to him to show me the light when I was under the swimming pool's surface. I had practiced my religion through my grade school years, completing the sacraments of Holy Communion, Penance, and Confirmation, but I lacked the dedication of these Catholic rites of passage through my life. Intellectually, I learned about my faith and God but grew to understand that their importance lies in their relationship with me. The university reawakened my living a life with God. My faith became the only relationship that never caused anxiety, frustration, or loneliness for me. God was another connection I acknowledged. God was home.

It was time to go back to my apartment. In a lingering moment, I recited words of thanks. The pause gave me the opportunity to see how the chapel was nestled in the center of a few encircling birch trees. God had spoken. I would forever be held by birch trees in thought and God in spirit.

I was learning more about this university, my relationship with it, and its tenets for life, one that included a spiritual blessing where my faith gave birth to a new connection. I didn't need the Catholic Church to grant me my religious identification or give me permission to call myself a person of faith. I no longer needed to feel guilty about not going to Mass every Sunday or giving up something for Lent or repenting judiciously on the holiest days of the year. I did not have to follow the traditional Catholic ways to confirm my loyalty or commitment. My relationship with God and prayer defined me as a spiritual being who had faith in something greater. I came to understand how I fit into faithful living, not how faith fit me. My belief was my own, and through God, I learned more about myself. And it was personal. I turned toward God, my God who I believed wouldn't let anything bad happen to me.

I would miss the views of center campus, realizing I would be there for only one more year. Reflection was automatic, as if a switch turned whenever I sat in the only chair in my apartment to watch a pulse of student traffic shuttle in and out while looking out at my world. I had my own square footage, and I counted my blessings in silent meditation. But soon I realized I had no place to go for the summer. *Where do I belong? Where do I go from here?* Dad was living in South Carolina with Selma, his fourth wife, (Laurie had died of cancer), in a house he had built along the thirteenth hole of a golf course. Visiting him was like being in a stranger's house and living with my mother would be stepping back when I had moved forward.

So I stayed in Milwaukee that summer and moved to the Saint James Apartments, a 1930s vintage building complete with caged elevator. My new apartment was large, with three spacious bedrooms to house four roommates, a dining room, kitchen, and even a small balcony. It was a welcome change from being alone in 425 square feet to spending my last year with friends.

During the summer, I worked evenings doing data entry of insurance claims, which left entire days open to find something, anything, to do. I would walk miles just to the grocery store, stroll around the empty campus, sit in the public library, wander through Italian Fest at the lakefront. Because I had no friends to distract me, I had ample time to think too much and then think about things a little bit more, and then maybe I'd analyze the whole thing again. Inactivity and gaps in time left me open to a wandering mind.

I often sat on my balcony after eating dinner. I would look at the stars and wish upon them and write in my journal under a glowing moonlight while listening to the city noises. There would be unusual darkness in a city. Then I'd look up to see the glow of the city lights bursting against an ashen sky. I was assured when I saw a glimmer of light that the heavens were trying to tell me there was light out there, really there was.

My observations were not limited to skies above and

streets below. A rustling of leaves diverted my attention as something uncharacteristic for a cityscape. In the corner of the balcony, slender tree limbs had grown, extending their reach over the deck. I walked closer to have a look. I recognized the leaves and the wispy branches flowing from a trunk of peeling bark. A birch tree! I felt its aloneness, standing in the corner of the alley and overgrown in shape. We had our spots to be, and we were making the best of where we were and what we had.

Jeff, a business student, lived upstairs. He had a motorcycle. He wore a black leather jacket and blue jeans, and his black curly hair escaped from his helmet but never waved in the wind while he rode his bike. A black moustache outlined his upper lip, and with every burst of laughter, his upper body wriggled and his smiling cheeks perked up, crushing his brown eyes shut. He would pull around to the back alley of the apartment and run the engine hard until I walked out and paid attention to him with a wave hello. *Just like in the movies*, I thought.

"Hey, how are you?" he'd yell up to me. "You want to come out and play? It's a great night. Just a quick ride?"

I was down the back stairs before he could pull out the extra helmet.

"I'm surprised you're out. You are always studying, trying to make the best grades for grad school."

"I am and you're right. That is and will be my focus. I don't have time for anything else except this one ride so shut up and hop on."

"You can actually ride one of these things?"

"Now hold on to my waist."

"What happens if I hold on too tight? If I squeeze tighter will we go faster?" I said.

"I'm not answering that."

"Hey . . . look . . . check out—"

"That moon, it's huge, it's so bright against the black sky."

"It's so big you can almost see its different shades of color."

Bike rides under the stars, and sharing study breaks at night all contributed to a relationship I didn't understand. I knew he had a girlfriend, but he never spoke about her. "I just find our friendship so refreshing," he said to me.

On Valentine's Day, I received a card under my door. Jeff's personal note ended with, ". . . and you saw the moon too," referring to the serendipitous moment on the motorbike. I left it at that.

Later that week he called.

"Hi . . . Jeff? Are you sick? You sound so quiet," I asked urgently.

"No."

"What's wrong?"

"I got my, my . . . Can you . . ."

I hung up the phone and ran up a flight of stairs in a panic to his apartment. The front door was open. Alley lights cast dim shadows in an already-dark room, where I could barely see Jeff's outline sitting slumped on the floor. I ran to him. "Are you okay?" He looked at me, nodded. He couldn't talk. A runny nose matched his weepy eyes.

"My god, what happened?" I asked.

"I didn't get the grade."

"It's about a grade? Did you fail?"

"No."

"Well, then, what's the problem?"

"It dropped my GPA," he yelled.

I didn't know what effect a lowered GPA had on admittance to grad school, if any. I wondered if he was being too dramatic.

I offered him a hug and a hand to hold, but the consolations didn't work. So I thought I'd sit with him, up against the wall, for a while longer, in silence.

I was sorry for Jeff, and I hoped I could do something to make him feel better. I wished I could take us back to those moments on his motorcycle, where the endless black night and glowing moon made us feel limitless and unburdened, unlike other nights sitting on my balcony when my birch tree and I felt our limitations. We were stuck in the wrong spot as we tried to make the best of where we were. But I couldn't. I knew he had to go through what was necessary to get what he wanted and where he wanted to be, just like me. We both had our moments, and this was one of them for Jeff. "I'm glad you called me. Thank you for thinking of me," were the only words I whispered to him.

"I don't know what I can do for you," I added.

"It's okay. Go. I'll be okay," he said softly.

The new year arrived. I needed self-confidence like any warrior needed armor. But in retrospect, I thought I had come a long way since my first year. When I glanced at my student ID picture, I saw a young woman with round oversized eyeglasses, a toothy smile with dimples, and brown cropped hair framing an innocent face. Just my head shot told you that the rest of me, all five foot three, 118 pounds, was petite and easily overlooked in a crowd. But now I saw myself evolving from a speechless schoolgirl to an inquisitive, driven young professional who maybe wasn't going to be easily overlooked after all. I was learning to connect to myself, to trust that I would figure out who I was and that God hadn't let anything bad happen to me.

defining moments

Defining moments highlighted my senior year. I had heard older, middle-aged adults talk about their defining moments, so I considered these would not happen until I got older, say, in my thirties! I thought I was on the right track when I was twenty-two, albeit a little early in life, because of my defining moments. They became noted markers that let me see my growth's progress like a child's standing up against a wall to be measured against a yardstick.

My first revelation happened in my advertising class, where we had to create an advertising campaign for a final project. I was a business manager on the team for the campaign because I had a knack for seeing the big picture and pulling necessary elements together to present a detailed, attractive package. This automatic inclination came naturally and granted me confidence. I considered my discovered talent and interest a sign that signified a direction to pursue after graduation.

Additional moments were surprises that called just as I was knocking on the door.

"I need to start class with an announcement, if you can just listen up for a minute here," Professor Lynn said. He was a fifty-something Ad Campaigns teacher, one of the best, I thought, who looked like everyone's dad, with his pipe smoking and casual dress to match his attitude. He would always look straight at you and hesitate for a moment when responding to a question posed to him, then answer it with a smile.

With pipe in hand, he started class. "I received a letter from Thompson Recruitment Advertising, they're right here, just up the street from us, a small agency that specializes in recruitment ads," the professor continued, "and they have an opening in their office for someone to work part-time as an intern. I also want to add that this is the first-ever offer this college has had for an internship with an outside company. So whoever gets this opportunity could be a real trendsetter here."

"I'll take it," I said, raising my hand. I felt the students' gazes on me.

Professor Lynn handed me the letter.

"It's an opportunity," he said. "Good luck."

My credibility as a student and as a new working professional was defined by my professor's announcement to the class. His confidence in me showed in his smile and a chuckle that worked in unison with his pipe-smoking rhythms.

A defining moment followed when I got the job. It didn't matter that I was an unpaid intern reading newspapers and cutting out tear sheets and answering a ringing phone, because for a couple mornings a week I wasn't a student but a working professional as I embraced the rhythm of the small recruitment advertising office. My defining moments were events that left lasting impressions. I had yet another place to be.

In early May, as the school term neared its end, it was time to leave the university. I was nervous about my exit interview at the J-school because I didn't know what it was or what to expect. It seemed so final, so abrupt, as if I had to sign out with a final act of permanence. I think my hesitancy was excitement in disguise, an indication the end had arrived and all my hard work, my experiences, and my struggles to be on my own had come together. The interview contained the ingredients for success and a map for the future.

I met Professor Lynn in a small office next to the stairwell on the second floor in the J-school.

"How are you doing?" he asked, taking a chair next to me. A soft, yellow-orange glow from an old desk lamp was the only light on our faces.

"I'm fine. Glad and yet sad that it's all over. It seems there still should be more, more to study, more to learn, more questions to ask. But I guess we're done," I said as a statement but thinking it was a question. I was trying to convince myself it was really over.

He was no longer my teacher or mentor. He wasn't sitting in front of me, but next to me. He had a talk with me, not at me. It was a shift in learning and a new meaning to the idea of *graduate.*

"How will you go about looking for a job?"

"I've got the Redbook directory to make a list of agencies, and I'm going to send out my résumé to as many agencies as I can for an entry-level position. I'll start with Leo Burnett, of course."

"Nancy, you've come a long way and you've really demonstrated your capabilities for all of us on the faculty. We've gotten to know you well over four years, and what we've seen is special. We are all so excited and proud. Your personality and creative journalistic sense will carry you to where you want to go. You've got what it takes, Nancy." I yearned to hear this. I craved the validation. And I got both.

In sharing this assessment with me, he validated me as a unique gem they had unearthed. I was ready for graduation. I had made it.

I walked out of the office with bittersweet emotions and tears of sadness mixed with happiness I had never known before. My escalating heartbeat accompanied me through the halls to the front door of the J-school, and a sudden montage of the past years gave birth in my head. I had played catch-up for four years, where I'd experienced high school while at college, enveloping new experiences and challenges of being an adult. This had been my place with brothers and sisters and teachers who instructed, encouraged, and challenged me. I discovered a world that wasn't in textbooks as assigned reading. My world advanced and expanded and was now open to anything. I learned to love life with the opening of the old faded blue wooden doors of the J-school.

Each defining moment built upon the one before it. Conviction gave me confidence to succeed in my school advertising project, and I could not have imagined myself having a different part. I was meant to be that business manager then, and I understood that was what I was to do in the future. My nervous excitement over an interview with my mentors was exacerbated by my lack of expectation and preparedness. The validation that I was headed to the right place to do the work I was meant to do negated my uneasiness. I was prepared with the knowledge I needed to swing doors open, and I believed I could do anything I wanted to. I could interview for a job, I could do a job well, and I would be prepared for what lay ahead. Most importantly, I had demonstrated a belief in myself, my connection to me.

My world had offered me connections, hope, wisdom, and grace. I viewed them as bridges to get me to a new place that offered opportunities to learn more about myself and to expand my vision of life. The connections enabled me to move forward.

Later that week, I took my last final. I closed my blue book and hesitantly handed it in, triggering flashbacks of the past four years narrated in white pages bound by blue covers and, in the end, finality and lasting impressions. I took photographs of the moments and filled the book of memories in my head, focusing on the details with each slow step—the crowded room of test-takers; stale, warm air; silence broken by a sneeze and a yawn—the flush in my cheeks, and the concentration in my brows.

I walked down the hall as if in slow motion, eyeing the double doors. When I came to the end, I paused. An echo from the swing of doors signaled the beginning of the end as metal banged shut to a finality of four years. My defining moments were brought to an end, but really, they were my beginning.

My heart palpitated as I stood on the top step of the J-school. I didn't know where to go or what to do. I didn't have any studying to do. It wasn't time to eat. I didn't have to stop at anyone's place. I had no plans. What was I going to do now? The answer was in my distraction, in the best part of my day, late afternoon, with the sun lowering in a dimming sky, cast in yellowish-pink, and looking innocent and fresh. Even though May signaled spring and hope for warmer weather, a cool dampness hung in the air. Just like any signal on cue, my heavy heart was calmed.

And then my contemplation broke.

An idling car and a loud voice broke my meditation. A white Opal was parked at the curb. Jeff jumped out of the car and ran up the three front steps of the J-school to meet me.

"I told you to call me when you were done," he said.

"I just finished. I'm thinking how it's really over. No more, yet there should be more. Isn't there always more?"

"There is, but sometimes not right away. Time and patience, my dear. And this is for you," Jeff said as he presented me with a single yellow rose. We hugged and laughed, and I cried. "I'm so glad I'm here, right now. Thank you," he said.

I valued his friendship. He brought me out of being serious to being spontaneous and living life. He was a crazy man, and I loved it, and I loved him for it.

J-school graduation arrived and departed as quickly as my four years were spent. The only ceremonial characteristic about it was joining the line to walk onstage to receive my diploma. I didn't exactly feel exuberant with the pomp and circumstance, the celebration before a grand entrance into the adult world to make something of my life and be a representative of my generation. Better suited for those overachievers, I thought. I didn't need to succumb to the pressure of trying to catch up to others or to be just like them. I derived my own self-confidence from believing I would evolve at my own pace, separate from the crowd, starting from my own beginning. My perspective was on a smaller scale, a selfish take on a milestone delivered upon completion of four years of scholastic and social maturity. It was personal self-satisfaction.

After the ceremony was over, I invited Mom and Dad to the apartment to join my three roommates and their families for a small gathering, an invitation I prefaced with, "You know, you really don't have to come. It was a long ceremony, and you could drive back if you feel you need to." I tried for selfish reasons to give them an excuse to leave, because I really didn't want to have to explain them to others. My divorced parents weren't like other parents, celebrating their child's dedication, hard work, and success in getting her degree. Their lack of excitement about me and the occasion was the antithesis of the celebratory atmosphere. On the outside, Mom was a fashion statement of perfection with her hair neatly coifed and wearing a fitted, crisp, new summer silk dress in the best shade of blue to complement her ivory skin tone. Her shoes and handbag matched. She was together, and she stood in confidence with an air of stiffness, perhaps because of the awkward situation. I saw her as a person without a match, standing in solitude on the inside where others were grouped in twos. I would never know her in any other way.

This look reminded me of a snapshot of her taken when I was about ten or twelve. Mom was seated on a black wrought iron chair on the patio in the backyard on Carlisle with her legs crossed and wearing a sky-blue polyester pantsuit. She was smiling in her Jackie-O black sunglasses with neatly coiffed dark brown, tightly permed hair. With an elbow on the armrest and one hand in the air, she held a lit cigarette between her fingers. The other hand held a plastic cup containing a light-colored beverage. She was a statement back then, and she carried it with her like an ID badge which never loses its place on the lapel.

Dad sat in an old, worn chair in the corner of the dining room, away from others, looking uncomfortable, as if he didn't belong there. The sun had faded low in the afternoon, casting shadows on him. I was looking at a stranger in the empty room, much like when I was a young girl watching him playing his drums in the basement, never quite making a connection. We didn't connect here either.

"Your father is hungry. Do you have anything to make a sandwich, or just a snack?" his wife, Selma, asked me.

"A sandwich? Now? Well, um . . . I don't know. I mean,

we don't have much to eat, we're all moving out this week, but let me see what I can do."

I hurried into the kitchen through the swinging doors. *I can't believe this. I'm with my friends, celebrating, trying to enjoy my day, and Dad needs a sandwich, now?* Mom, Dad, and Selma stood with awkward and forced conversation. They didn't have any idea who or what I had become, so I figured they didn't really know what to celebrate.

"Here you go. Is this okay? Peanut butter and jelly is all I have. Sorry. But it should hold you over till you get back."

"Well, we'll be going soon, anyway," Selma said.

Then why don't you just go now, just leave if you are so painfully unhappy and feel so out of place that you can't join the others and show your daughter how proud and happy you are? I stood next to Dad until he finished. Then it was time to go, and I walked them out to the car.

"Okay, well, I'll see you. Thanks for coming, and drive back safely," I said.

Now alone, I didn't want to go back and join an apartment full of people, because I knew I might have to explain my parents' behavior and why they'd left so soon. I wanted everyone to go home. I wanted this day to be about me, to give myself the needed recognition and pride that I had made it. My lack of connection with my parents in that room was evident. Strange, how a sad realization solidified my proud sense of who I had become.

I thought about my childhood years living on Carlisle, knowing my birch buddy was just outside the front door. Back then, I never thought my tomorrows would be any different from living the current moments. That child in me had been resurrected and transplanted to a new home, where my life's vision was building for my new future. One year had followed the next, and the motion had progressed automatically. I had had classes to attend and schedules to maintain for four years. But then the motion stopped.

My readiness to graduate was only insofar as I was

equipped with what any twenty-two-year-old needed to navigate the outside world—a college degree and confidence. But I was in transition, where I still needed the connections from my university home. I would remember my classes, O'Donohue's on Friday night, Tombstone pepperoni pizza from the dorm store at midnight after returning from O'Donohue's, live concerts in the Mug Rack on a Friday afternoon where I, alone, enjoyed being in my world.

Separating myself from these many connections was not easy. It had taken years to establish the links that enabled me to learn about myself and where I wanted to be. Creating the links could not be forced or rushed. I learned to trust and believe that my connections were there for a reason—to teach, to follow, to study, to reinforce the person I was discovering. Even though I was entering a new world, post-graduation, I allowed myself the time and gave myself permission to be alone and to trust that God would not let anything bad happen to me. I had become strong enough to rely on my courage and resiliency when I thought I had none of it when I started college. My connections were not only to home, but were vehicles to move forward.

transitions

As campus emptied for summer break, I thought I should be there too, walking through the center of campus where I criss-crossed daily to and from classes and ended my day at the J-school on Wisconsin Avenue. It was my home; I belonged there. Without it, I was afraid I would regress to a place void of connection, leaving me in limbo, alone, with no direction.

I sat on a cement bench mounted just off to the side of center campus watching a trickling of students and the quieting of campus life as the term ended. As my eyes engaged with the rhythm of the walkers, the familiar sight of two grown birch trees stopped my attention. Their swaying branches and rustling leaves stood in the distance next to the St. Joan of Arc chapel, guarding the historic, sacred spot, much like my birch tree had anchored me at my house on Carlisle. I was reminded that comfort from home and my Jesuit school and teaching would always be with me as they became one and the same. I breathed, deeply invoking my faith. This was my home; I belonged somewhere.

I had everything I needed to start my new life. But I didn't know where to begin. I had to free my self-confidence and personality as well as the ability to sell myself to any prospective employer. I needed to open my mind to venture into a new world where I had to start over, introducing myself to others where no one would know my name. I understood intellectually that I was supposed to get out and find a job in my field now that I had graduated, but my heart and my head told me otherwise, as they were in different places. I rented a studio apartment, my decompression chamber, on Sixteenth Street for the summer, and I gave myself permission to park there for a while. I tried to convince myself that some direction or inspiration or both would be bestowed upon me as the result of living alone in a small apartment on the outskirts of campus. Staying in Milwaukee was an enabling act that made me feel I was still a part of a happy life, in denial of the fact that the life I had come to know had ended.

I occupied every moment of subsequent summer days with walking until I couldn't complete another step. I tired easily. As I slowed my pace, I watched mothers holding one baby on their hip while squeezing a toddler's hand with their other as they muscled their way on and off the city bus. Male office workers briskly walked with briefcase in one hand, grabbing the ties that blew over their shoulders when the winds gusted. These travelers had a purpose in their gait, and they were on their way. *Did I have a purpose? Where was I headed?*

As summer came to an end, I had neither school nor a

job waiting for me. I was lost, and homeless, as my apartment would have new tenants soon. I did have a place to go, though—back to the townhouse with my mother—my only viable option. I had no other choice; I had run out of them.

A couple of weeks before I was to leave Milwaukee, I needed to check out the Redbook and compile a mailing list of all the ad agencies in Chicago as a reference for sending out my résumé once I returned home. Then I had to pack for the trip to Mom's place. I piled my belongings in the center of the apartment, considered what I could part with, and saw there wasn't much. Tim was picking me up in a borrowed neighbor's station wagon, and the longer I waited for him, the more time I had to think about what remained after four years. And then I cried. I cried as I mourned the life of the innocent and naive freshman I once had been and the people who became my friends. I cried for those relationships that never went where I wanted them to go. I cried because I missed my inspirational family of journalism students. I cried because I was alone again and moving away from another place I had made my home.

I had been wrapped in structure with classes, and now I had no schedule to dictate my life. I was stripped, and I knew absolutely nothing.

The buzzer interrupted my internal struggle.

"Tim?"

"Yeah, it's me. What floor?"

"Second." I buzzed him in. I met him at my door.

"You've got all this? It all won't fit. Some of it you'll have to leave," he said, working his way to the middle of the room.

"Just stop and let's start moving out," I said. I grabbed boxes and suitcases, and Tim followed with my television and record player.

I made it all fit, including the daybed, within the confines of the old station wagon with some smart packing and patience, none of which Tim could claim. We were on our way with blasting music competing with a knocking engine. I said goodbye one last time in my thoughts. I carried with me a well-earned spirit that I prayed would not leave me once I went back in time.

elle

I took refuge that summer at a too-familiar place, the townhouse. As much as I had clenched my jaw and raised my shoulders to my ears in tension before walking in the door, I had no reason to do so. My move back was seamless. I had seen how Mom managed her days and her household, handling on her own the paying of bills and other chores. In my absence, she had learned to rely on herself. Perhaps I would be just fine too when it came to relying on myself to handle whatever came my way.

Where I had once sought distraction while lying spread-eagle on a sun-warmed towel on hot cement, I had returned to reclaim and acknowledge additional connections I had made when I was away. When comparing my links—those made before college with those made during—I saw I had come a long way in growth and maturity.

The sound of splashing water surrounded me poolside with now-overgrown wild prairie. I listened to the symphony of crickets chirping in rhythm with the water's ripple. The wind carried sweet smells of wildflowers, chlorine, and humid air. The clubhouse held on to its new wood smell with accompanying mounds of wood chips surrounding its mature landscaping. I was transported back in time when I once had connected with place, sounds, and smells.

"Hello, how are you?" My eyes diverted to the lifeguard standing in front of me.

"Hi. Just fine, thanks," I answered. I sat up on my elbows to get a better look behind the voice. "Not real busy this morning, huh?"

"No, not yet. This afternoon," he said. He pulled up

a lounge chair next to me, bringing with him a smell of chlorine and sunscreen.

"I'm Scott."

"Nancy. I live across the street. This is your first summer here?"

"Yep. I'm staying with my parents, until the fall when I go to law school in Tampa."

I noted how he didn't say, "living at home," but rather, "staying with my parents." Perhaps we understood that where we lived was a stop along the way to get where we wanted to be, a home base that was ours and not someone else's."Law school, huh?" I chuckled. *Damn. Those law guys trailed me from college.*

"And you? What about you?"

"I graduated, moved back with my mother, and I'm looking for a job in advertising." I realized the total summation of my life at the age of twenty-two was bound by this three-action statement.

"Good luck. You'll do fine."

"I'm glad someone thinks so."

I figured he was married or otherwise attached to someone. He was too good-looking, too poised, too everything. But sometimes he appeared sad or just not there. I wondered if our minds were in similar spheres. His smile was offset by his sex appeal: tanned, slender body and green glowing eyes. He was mysterious and not a man of many words; he would sometimes chuckle and smile for no reason I could discern. But he did have a knack for finding the humorous. His sarcasm was always well-timed. I thought we might have this in common.

"So, how did you get this lifeguard gig, anyway?" I asked.

"Long story. Just a word-of-mouth thing," he said, letting out a burst of laughter. "Being a lifeguard is not my calling, you know."

I didn't think it was, I thought. I smiled at him.

Going to the pool took on a new meaning for me, as

it wasn't just about going for a swim and relaxation anymore. I went to see Scott. Though our conversations were limited, understandably because his job was to watch others and not me, evenings provided slow time for us to get to know each other. Our conversations were lighthearted with laughter between our responses and dry humor getting us through our seemingly similar situations.

"Not going to law school, here, in the city?" I asked.

"Hell no, I hate the cold. Won't be staying here during the winter, that's for sure. How can you stand it here in the winter?"

"I don't know any different. Besides, I'm young and adapt to my surroundings, unlike you, perhaps?" I didn't know exactly how much older Scott was, but I used the mystery as a conversation prodder. "I have to stay with my mom while I'm looking for a job in the city."

"Well, looks like we're both getting to where we want to be."

"Yep, and sitting poolside, relaxing through the rest of the summer is the way to get there, isn't it?" I agreed.

Our poolside conversations shifted to the telephone and seeing each other away from the pool. Soon, my dates with Scott were just as I imagined real dates should be. We would start our evening with a cocktail at Andy's, a small, dark, jazz piano bar, then head over to Spiazza for an Italian dinner, sitting shoulder-to-shoulder in tall black booths with white tablecloths, and finally on to the Rafaella to hear piano jazz as we sipped aperitifs. We would walk down Oak Street, then to the beach. Our conversations protected us from thinking about the reality of where we were in our lives.

We sat at the pool one Thursday night looking ahead to when we would be getting together again.

"Elaine and Clay wanted to know if we'd like to go to brunch with them at the club this Sunday," he said. I noted how he referred to his parents by their first names.

"Sounds great. And then we've got the Bears game the next weekend. I'm looking forward to that day. I've never been to a Bears game."

"You've lived here all your life and you've never been to a Bears football game?"

"Can't say that I have . . ."

We lacked the seriousness that should automatically progress with a relationship. But what we lacked in closeness through conversation we gained in carefree spirits, allowing us to just have fun.

One date night, he wouldn't tell me where we were going. I was happily surprised when we landed at the 94th Aero Squadron, a quaint restaurant with French chalet decor, circa WWI, and dining room windows that overlooked the Palwaukee Airport runways. We were uninhibited enough, thanks to having shared a bottle of wine, to run away with our desires and act on spur-of-the-moment inclinations. Just when I thought we were headed to the car, he grabbed my hand, and we made a dash for an open field, joining the view of the restaurant diners. Tall grass slowed our pace in the kohl-black night. We whispered conversation so as to not break the eerie silence. Suddenly, lights flickered. A loud running engine noise broke. "Get down," he yelled. We plunked to our bellies. "Here one comes." Within seconds a private plane skimmed over our backs and glided to the runway. I screamed at the thrill of it. He joined in laughter and then more screams. We were holding on to the present moment and enjoying life and each other.

Dating Scott was enabling my lack of dedication to my job search and allowing me to succumb to résumé rejection. Our busy social outings and the knowledge he would be leaving once the pool closed kept at bay my expectations about our relationship and what we were to each other. By the fall, I still hadn't worked toward finding a job, but I didn't even care that I had defied my guilt—I was with someone to enjoy my summer.

Then, one mid-September morning, Scott called and asked me to meet him for lunch. My heart pounded with worry as he greeted me with a dozen yellow roses. *Is this a bad thing? If so, why is he trying to make me feel good?*

He started off our conversation, "You know how I started part-time work at the law firm in the city? Well, they offered me a full-time job."

"Okay, so, what are you saying?" I said.

"I'm taking the job and will be staying here."

"No law school in Florida?"

"Nope. I'm going to stay in Chicago and be just as miserable as you with the god-awful winter weather."

I didn't know what to make of this statement, given that accepting a job in the city was in conflict with his adamant intention to move. This shift of intention and his giving me flowers confused me. I reasoned that time would explain, so I resolved to let the situation play out.

As the weeks progressed, Scott's full-time job was all-consuming, leaving him tired and unenthused. Our time together became limited.

"How about we go out on Saturday, a walk somewhere to enjoy this fall weather and then dinner out?" I asked him one Friday afternoon.

"Saturday? As in tomorrow?"

"Yes. But, you look as if you couldn't possibly think about tomorrow when all you want to do is get through the afternoon."

"I'll be here at work, late. I'll call you tomorrow."

I knew he wouldn't, and he didn't. And I let it go. There was nothing I could do. As the fall gave way to winter's cold and gray skies, I sensed that our relationship was fading. One night, as we were driving home from a date in the city, he said just above a whisper, "We could dream and wish and take ourselves anywhere." Staring ahead, he added, "I'm crazy about you, but, we . . . we, have no future."

My heart pounded, and my cheeks flushed. I didn't say

anything. We continued driving through the city, meeting stoplights, and slowly starting up again as Handel played on the car stereo. "I could see you working in the city and fitting right in." He had it all figured out for me, but I didn't want him to. "And probably forgetting about me," he added.

"Are you mad at me?" he asked.

"No."

But I was mad. I was mad because good things that happened to me seem to desert me, and he was a good thing. I was mad because he was calling the shots, and it was out of my control. *Why doesn't anything work out for me?* My anger mingled with sadness.

We stopped at a traffic light on Michigan Avenue, and he pointed to a Saks Fifth Avenue store window at the corner. "See, over there, with the winter coats, the one in the middle, tan, big buttons, big collar. I like that one. I could see you in that with a pink cashmere scarf around your neck. You're so very mature. I think about you and wonder about you. You look like you belong in one of those Camay soap commercials." He smiled. The drive was completed in silence.

His attention to me diminished as I found him to be more impersonal, isolating himself from his usual social interests.

I stopped by to see Scott on a Saturday before Christmas.

"Hi there. How are you doing?" I asked, looking directly in his face to take my own measurement of his wellbeing. He was pale and looked tired, with shadows under his hazel eyes. The smile I had grown accustomed to seeing whenever he greeted me was gone.

"Oh, just great, splendid," he said sarcastically.

"I have a Christmas present for you. What are you doing for the hol—"

"No, I don't want a present," he interrupted, his raised voice drowning out my question.

I looked down at the box and remembered how creatively I'd turned a nondescript shirt box into a festive holiday package, carefully surrounding the best wool sweater I had been able to find in his favorite color. Perhaps I thought my kind gesture and dose of niceness would heal him and make him want to be with me. "I want nothing," he said as he pushed the gift back into my hands. "Listen, I don't have any plans for Christmas but to be alone while Elaine and Clay are in Florida." The defiance in his tone startled me. He was angry. I didn't recognize who he was, who he had become. "C'mon now, take this back. It's really time—"

"But I want you to have it, it's Christmas, and . . . " My voice faded as he stepped closer to me to put his hands on my shoulders, turn me around, and walk me out the door.

"Thanks, but really, I don't want presents. I don't want a thing," he said, standing in the doorway as I was pushed outside.

I paused to consider the confrontation. At best, I'd expected a calm and civil chat to follow his rejection that clearly had indicated a breakup. But then I remembered how we never really talked about where we were in our lives and our relationship. I wondered what we really had been to each other. I didn't have an answer.

I don't remember speaking to him after that incident. We weren't to be together anymore.

I thought how my young-girl self would have spoken in frustrated angst, how nothing works out for me and nobody wants to be with me. I had attributed this to an innate flaw, something I lacked, an underdevelopment that would eventually be the cause of the disconnection. But my big-girl self had grown out of that reflection and saw the connections as links to move my self-understanding along.

Scott was the bridge that enabled me to leap from a life I had grown into, giving me a sense of security, to reach the other side, and to plant an attitude that would push me on my way. It wasn't meant to be anything long-term; it was a short-term investment, where I valued the time and reaped the rewards.

It would take the remaining winter months and into the spring for me to get serious about getting a job and moving out of my mother's place. Once I realized this, a new door would open after this one had shut.

ellce

I refocused my intention to have a job soon, but not just any job; it had to be one in advertising. My best talent was myself, and I knew it. My spirit would not be broken, as I believed each day would get me closer to employment. I remembered the college days, where God and faith sustained my belief that nothing bad would happen to me.

On a whim, I answered a nondescript ad in the paper. It was a blind response in that I didn't know what the job was. I was offered an interview.

"Well, by now, you are probably wondering what company this is for, right?" the female headhunter asked. She held the last bit of information in suspense until I first qualified.

"Well, yes, I am."

"The job that I need to fill is for a traffic assistant."

"I'm sorry. I'm not really familiar with traffic in an ad agency."

"This position is in the broadcast department, where commercials for television and radio get scheduled . . . and the agency is Leo Burnett," she said in drawn-out words.

"Leo Burnett?"

"Yes, they're in the city, in the Prudential building." I had a flashback to my college exit interview, when I'd told my professor I would start there. I believed it would happen then, and it did now. My conviction was fulfilled, and I couldn't help smiling and thinking this was meant to be.

When the elevator opened its doors on my interview day, Leo Burnett's well-known large signature in shiny steel covered the wall ahead of me. This wasn't just a leading ad agency I was in the midst of; it was an agency that considered me good enough to work there. Even though I hadn't had the interview just yet, I was convinced that this was my place to be and that I would have the job.

I accepted the job offer the following day from my soon-to-be manager. The acceptance was more validation, a starting point from which to branch out and thrive. Once again, I recognized that God didn't let anything bad happen.

I started working at the best, most sought-after advertising agency in the fall of 1984.

part 4

a second decade

working it out

I relished my work routine at Burnett for only a year before bouts of anxiety surfaced. Something was missing or just not right. I'd start my day with a positive attitude, but by the end of it I was asking, "What the hell am I doing?" Was this a normal feeling for a twenty-three-year-old? I was coasting when I should have been gaining speed in my career. Those who asked me where I worked were surprised, even envious when I told them. Their excitement made me think that I should be grateful to have a job in a special place, and that I should value my seat among professionals. However, they didn't know just how low I was on the ad-agency hierarchy. Though their responses made me feel lucky, it was a temporary feeling.

Am I to be here for the rest of my working life? What's next for me? The agency business was difficult, competitive, and over-supplied with eager, aggressive players pushing to get picked for the next level. I wasn't one of them but I stuck to my thoughts that someday, someone would notice me, and I would have an opportunity to move up in my career. *But when?*

The Advertising Club at my old J-school took a field trip to the city to visit a couple ad agencies, and Leo Burnett was one of them. An account executive walking through the door interrupted me as I was talking to the students about how I got my job. He explained his agency position—account executive—and I was hooked. I wanted to be an account executive just like him. I, too, wanted to work with clients and come up with ideas and sell them. I wanted to write strategies and deliver the goals. But I had no idea how to get there. The wheels in my head started in motion.

A goal served as a link to a vision of a place I wanted to be with a position I sought to hold. I had the goal, but did I have the steps mapped out to get me there? I could only value the achievement and trust that the path I needed to take to get me there would work itself out. God wasn't going to let anything bad happen to me.

After a year of employment, I moved out of my mom's place, southeast, to a studio apartment in Evanston, where I had quick access to the city. My corner place was cheery with thick-paned windows spanning from the radiator tops to the ceiling, allowing light to flood inside. I doled out a few necessary furniture pieces to round out the corner: a bed, a bookcase, and a wrought iron café table and chairs. A long, cushy, hand-me-down couch stretched long to fill a wall opposite the windows. My tiny kitchen had a window that provided an escape for the cooking odors I excitedly stirred up.

A promotion to traffic coordinator after eighteen months kept me moving up in my department. I received a promotion to senior coordinator eighteen months later, managing coordinators. But the agency was too big for me, with its account-management training program and a male-dominated, highly educated force to match its size.

I reasoned I would need to leave the agency to get where I wanted to be.

At home, my empty, chameleon-like apartment reflected my mood and feelings, matching the outside as I looked through those panoramic windows and tried to connect and find my place to be. The windows were like looking glasses, mirroring a gray, cloudy day, a reflection of new aloneness that began to spread from outside to what I had once found to be bright and happy inside. I struggled to reconnect to that person.

My coworker Lorraine and I went to Clubland on the north side of the city one Friday night for drinks and dancing. I was distracted by a tall, slender, dark-haired guy standing next to me at the bar when we caught each other's stares. I smiled because I didn't know what else to do at that awkward moment. I noticed his nose wrinkled when he smiled at me.

On Monday morning Lorraine said, "Hey, Nancy, here, this is for you." She handed me a small piece of paper with a giggle behind her grin. "It's that guy's name and phone number from Friday night. Wow, you sure made an impression."

Flattery eased my doldrums and self-doubt. I called Pat later that morning; we met for lunch and talked as if we'd been friends for a long time, picking up where we'd left off. His warm conversation coincided with his soft-spoken words. His gentleness was attractive to me.

It was all about Pat that summer. My thoughts were about him, and I wondered when I would see him again. Admittedly, my zealous attitude was overbearing compared to his more relaxed, casual nature. I was full speed ahead. He was one date at a time.

On a warm August night, we set out on a date. His eyes locked on to mine after I opened my apartment door to welcome him.

"Hello to you, come on in," I said.

His faded blue jeans fit him well. He wore a white shirt, tails out, with a couple buttons undone at the top. His tan face and chest complemented his long black wavy hair and dark eyes.

I thought he was a rock star, and he was standing in *my* doorway.

The clapping echoes of my floppy sandals making contact with each stair broke the silence trapped in the stairwell. He had parked just outside the front doors.

When I was seated inside his black MG, I surveyed the tan interior and realized the top was down. My eyes were free to greet every star in the blue-black night sky and grab every sensory experience available—intermittent horns honking; the sweet smell of summer breezes, damp lake water, and pungent wildflowers; spots of colored lights against the soft tan and brown hues of apartment buildings. I was back to those summers of long ago sitting poolside during the best part of my day and learning to live in the moment while taking nothing for granted. When Pat caught me staring at him, we smiled at one other. I was a grownup reaching for a connection to a right place, a right time, with the right person, just as I was reaching for the stars as I sat in his car. My happiness calmed my nervous and anxious self as thoughts of not being in the right agency with the right job retreated from my mind.

After dinner, he drove around the lake's shore, where the water was calm, the air smelled of leftover sunscreen, and echoes of yelling and laughter subsided. The sand was cool under our feet when we stopped to talk.

"This has been a great evening. I enjoyed being with you. You're very attractive and funny," he said.

"Thanks for the ride in your car. I loved it."

"Was that the best part for you this evening?" He chuckled.

"Sure was. No, no, just kidding. I hope not, I hope there's still more evening left."

"You know, I . . . I don't know if I can handle another commitment," he said.

Here we go again. This is it. I won't see him again.

"I don't mean to pressure you . . . or . . . I just like being with you."

Pat and I continued to walk with arms entwined, stopping for kisses and hugs. Our hugs were more like desperate clingings, lasting long enough to dismiss his fears and my anxiety about the possibility this would be our last date. I thought it was over with my rock star before it even got started. The drive home was more serious than the drive that started the evening, but our exchanged glances and smiles reassured me that maybe it wasn't as bad I thought; or maybe I chose denial.

I was curious about exactly what Pat did for a living, as I associated his shaggy dark hair, diamond earring, and rolled-up sleeves with being an artist or other creative type.

One summer night, I stood in his kitchen—a kitchen by name, not by design.

"So, you work in the family's photo lab full-time?" I asked.

"I'm also in theater with a group. We perform at the Roxy on Fullerton. Now go on over to the fridge," he said.

"Okay, so what am I supposed to do now?"

"Open the freezer."

I opened the freezer and saw an arm that appeared to be cut off at the elbow sitting on top of a bag of frozen vegetables and a packaged T-bone. "Okay, so, there's an arm in your freezer . . . and you're keeping this on ice, frozen, for . . . what? To attach to the upper arm that is being worked on in the basement?"

"Yes, that's exactly what I'm doing," he chuckled. "I create special effects for movies and videos, you know . . . blood, gore, body parts, whatever they need." Showing me what he did for a living rather than telling me created its own special effect. My rock star won me over by showing me his fake body parts.

Pat walked down the kitchen stairs to the backyard

to corral his two plump bulldogs into the house for the night. I remained at the door, holding it open to watch him standing at the bottom of the cement stairs. I looked down at him and caught a dim doorway light casting a glow on his upper body. Pat joined me on the top step. I put my arm through his, looked at him, and closed my eyes to hold the moment. When I opened them he was staring at me. He put his arms around me, and we hugged.

"Charlotte Rampling. Do you know who she is? She's an actress. You look like her," he whispered.

"Yes, I do, in fact I just saw her in *The Verdict*. Mmm."

He pulled me to my feet and held me close. We stared long and kissed softly. His six-foot-two-inch frame towered over my five-foot-three-inch self. I followed him to a dark bedroom with only the lamplight from the living room casting a dim yellow glow on the bed. We lay down, embraced, kissing while entwined. He rolled on to his side gazing at me, close. My heart raced, and my cheeks flushed with excitement and anticipation.

"I want a picture of you," he said.

"A picture? Well, okay, sure. I'm not sure I've got a good one, but I'll see." I'd never been asked for a picture before. I giggled in the innocence of the question and delighted in giving him my response. "This would be my first time," I whispered. I was comfortable enough in the intimacy of the moment to admit my inexperience. And then I second-guessed my confession to presume this make-out session would lead somewhere.

And then all motion stopped, still, quiet. A pause.

"I can't do this, Nancy . . . no, just can't. I don't want to be the one, nope, no."

"Well, okay, then . . . well, I'll just go then? I guess I'll just go."

God, I didn't want him to answer that. I wanted him to say that everything was okay and to stay for a little while longer. My confession had stopped everything.

I stood, straightened myself, and stared at him, flushed with embarrassment, hoping he'd say he was sorry, that he didn't mean to push me away and to come close, back to him. I hurriedly said goodbye and walked out the front door. I couldn't remember where I'd parked, so I continued walking around the block with nothing but the previous conversation guiding my nomadic search. I was too young, naive, and embarrassed; I was that college student again. I was fun to be with and attractive, but I still couldn't get the boyfriend.

We didn't date or speak with each other often after that, but just when I reached a low point in professional and personal happiness, the Applebash, an employee-bonding event at the ad agency, rescued me. Employees enjoyed a day of barbecues and softball games in a carnival setting.

I had dressed in pink leggings and purple leotard, a fashion statement for the early eighties, for an aerobics dance session during the event.

"Hello there," Len said.

Len was older than I, maybe twenty years.

"Hi. Were you standing there the whole time? Were you watching us when you should have been working out with us?" I asked.

"Yes and no. I was standing there most of the time, and hell no, I wasn't going to do that stuff."

"Not a joiner, huh?"

"No way."

"So, what is it that you do, anyway?" I asked.

"I'm in programming."

"And that means?"

"Oh, c'mon, do we really have to talk about work stuff?"

"No, not at all, but I would like to talk to you more. I'm stuck in Traffic and want to get out."

"Understand. I'll call you."

While I was walking along the city street to meet him for lunch, I was fired up by a confidence boost because I was one of them, doing what other office workers were doing, breaking for lunch to talk business and getting to know colleagues outside of work.

Len stood up from his table and waved me over.

Dressed in a suit that echoed warm summer breezes—a soft blue linen pleated skirt and a long jacket I had made years earlier—I wore the flowing outfit well. The look on his face, as if a beam of light had fractured the dim dining room when I entered the restaurant, validated the impression I'd wanted to make.

"Thanks for having lunch with me. I really appreciate it. Just being able to talk to others outside the department is great. I'm trying to move to the next level."

"Should we order?" he said. "So, where are you living now?"

"I'm in Evanston. Moved from my mom's condo in Buffalo Grove."

"I'm not far from there, living with my two boys. I'm divorced."

"Well, my parents divorced when I was fifteen, and we had to sell our house in Deerfield. I had to grow up fast," I continued. "It really wasn't a big deal for me. Dad wasn't around much anyway, but then Mom had to get a job . . . "

"I understand."

"I'm just trying to get somewhere, to move up, make more money, have more fun."

"I'll help in any way I can."

During my first job out of college, I quickly rallied toward new opportunities. I thought I would get to where I wanted to be if I worked hard, networked with the right people, and proved my abilities. But my expectations fell short, and I turned to desperation by trying to impress this ad agency exec.

It wasn't about the guy who made fake body parts, though he had been a welcome surprise and an unregrettable experience. It was about craving validation that I could get to where I wanted to be, the attention that meant I wasn't

being overlooked, and the right personal and business connections to find my belonging, my home.

I continued to work it out.

fire only gets me so far

I was working six days a week at Burnett. On Saturdays,
I'd take the 9:20 morning train downtown and catch the
4:40 afternoon return. Working Saturdays in winter was an
exercise in stamina and will, because that was all I had to
get me through a car enveloped in frozen tundra. But as I sat
in my car waiting for the igloo to crack under subtle signs
of warming, I raised the volume on the radio and let the
mighty voice and drum beats of Chaka Khan pull me out of
the parking space and push me along in my Renault Fuego.
I depended on the Fuego—which means "Fire"—and its
spirit and energy for my newly acquired job with the top
rolled back on summer days and Bruce "The Boss" Springsteen belting out "Born in the USA." I needed the feeling
that I had control of something, even though it was just the
start of the Fire's ignition to get me to the train station.

But the Fire only got me so far. I acknowledged how
things were losing their stamina: the car's turbo engine, the
novelty of working for the best ad agency in the country,
and my mental and physical wellbeing.

As this new low surfaced, I turned to an open ear to
talk through my angst. One Monday morning I called Len.

"Hi. I thought I'd see what you were doing for lunch
today," I said.

"Nothin' but having you come up here," Len said. "I'll
have the popcorn going."

Just how does he know I need to talk?

I joined him in the screening room, a dark cocoon with
two two-seater leather couches in front of two television
monitors, a coffee table, and built-in bookcases housing

black VHS tape boxes. The room was soundproofed and secure, a good thing to know just in case I had emotional moments. I could smell the popcorn down the hall before I rounded the corner and snuck into the room undetected by others.

"Hey, how's it going?" he asked.

"Oh, you know, a little frantic and tense. What's going on with you?"

"Not much, going to New York tomorrow to talk to some big shots who believe they are big shots, but they aren't really. Forget that. What's on your mind? I can sure see something's there," he said in a whisper.

"I had my review. I was put on probation, and I don't know why. I don't understand this. How in the hell can they put me on probation when I've been promoted every year for the past three years? Doesn't that say something? I honestly don't know why," I said in a raised voice while holding back tears.

Len and I talked often; if not in the evening, he made a point to call me during the day. He could tell when I needed his ear. I made a mental note, acknowledging his kindness and endurance in keeping up with an unhappy person.

His voice on the telephone signaled to me a go-ahead for an emotional outpouring.

"Hi, it's me again," Len said.

"You're working late," I mumbled.

"I'm saying the same about you."

"You wanna come up?"

"Yes, but I don't need any popcorn."

I tried to keep it together because letting go in front of a man in his department was unprofessional. Len ushered me into the screening room and shut the door.

"I'm at the end of my thirty-day probation and I think I'm going to get fired," I said.

I held my head down. I looked at my lap, where my sweaty folded hands sat in a tidy knot.

I remembered when I knew I wanted to be in account management but realized I'd have to leave to get there. The push to find an agency and the right job was overwhelming. And here I was, in the process of being pushed out while counting on something better for me. But maybe it wasn't a matter of finding something. It was not a "something," but a believing in "it." What exactly was "it," though?

One Friday night, I went to see Pat in his show at the Roxy, a nightclub with a bar in one room and a small theatre in the other. We hadn't seen each other in months, but it didn't matter. I really sought comfort in the happiness I'd once known by connecting with him. When the spotlights cast down on him onstage, I noticed he had cut his hair and was wearing that small diamond earring I remembered. My rock star! Pat looked down at me and smiled as the cast lined up and took their bows. His smile was familiar, my connection.

I was seeking a secure place at a time when my insecurities and vulnerabilities were raw. The few hours' distraction granted me an escape to a time where I'd smiled often and giggled uninhibitedly. I was better only insofar as I realized how far I had come from reaching for the stars in Pat's car to now, when I was reaching for professional success. But I still didn't belong anywhere or with anyone.

I recognized Len as a friend who gave his every effort to make me happy and do anything he could to help me get what I wanted, but I failed to acknowledge it. I had validation and belonging in front of me, but I didn't embrace them, and I didn't know why. I was selfish because I was using him for support and comfort. I feared he would realize the only time I called him was when I needed attention and to complain and spew my unhappiness, my toxicity onto an otherwise happy and optimistic person. But no matter how much happiness he wanted to infuse in me, to get me where I wanted to be, he couldn't do it. He couldn't do it because I needed to do it myself.

Len remained my true friend, despite my inner turmoil and consistent drama as we continued to exchange phone calls.

thick skin

I spoke daily on the telephone with Cliff, a sales rep from outside the office. His calm voice was quiet, with a deep, slow cadence contrasting to the chaos surrounding me on my work floor. Though I had never met him, I imagined what he must look like—dark hair and eyes, polished, a strong and silent type—based on the tone of his voice.

One June afternoon, I attended a Cubs baseball game at Wrigley Field. Sitting under a blue umbrella sky with the sun warming the top of my head, I stared at center field where the confines met the ivy-covered redbrick wall. I could see forever. My desire to run and to fly into the sky and be caught by a cushioned wall gave me a renewed spirit to relax, breathe deeply, and roll with whatever pitch was thrown to me. The ballpark was a magical, happy place where spirits of competition came together and free wills were wrapped in a game that was so American.

As I sat there, I recognized a familiar voice.

"Hi, I'm Cliff."

"Hi. Nancy. And it's finally nice to meet you in person."

"Likewise."

"I didn't realize it was you who was sitting next to me. So, you are the one responsible for us being here? Thanks for the tickets."

Cliff was tall and well built, with curly dark blond hair and hazel eyes that squinted when he smiled, revealing a set of dimples that complemented his tan face. I chuckled at the thought of how he looked so different from the image in my imagination.

"So, do you keep a scorecard?" he asked.

"No, I've never done one before. But you look like you always do these things." I said, pointing to his filled-out card.

"No, never have. Just copied the batting lineup off the board over there. Looks like I know what I'm doing, though, doesn't it?"

"You look like a serious Cubs fan now, mister."

We quickly became best friends first—a marker before I could maybe, possibly, just perhaps call him a boyfriend. I had come a long way since my college days when I questioned if someone I'd just met could be a boyfriend before any friend-making could be developed. It had also been a long time since it wasn't always about my own drama.

I had expected challenges when making friends in the city, but when I met Cliff and our friendship continued outside work, I confirmed I'd met my marker. The ease with which this relationship progressed was affirming. We walked our city; stopped to visit Andy's, a jazz bar; and had dinners steeped in laughter and fun. However, one Sunday afternoon when we returned to my apartment after brunch, we couldn't come to an agreement on what to do next.

"Ugh. It's hot. The sun, it's in my eyes. I'm sweating, sticky," I moaned. "I can't just lie here. It's a stellar summer day. Let's do something. Let's take a walk."

"No, no, I don't want to walk," he said.

"Let's get over there," he said, pointing to the bed as if answering its call.

We lay spread-eagle on the firm surface. I anticipated his intention.

"Umm, this will be . . . my . . ." I said in a whisper, "my first time."

I braced for a halt. But he didn't stop. He didn't get up. He looked at me, smiled, revealing those dimples, and blushed. His affirming reaction made me realize that everything would be just fine.

"Well, I just thought you might want to know that . . ."

I felt silly about my declaration, as if my confession were

a prerequisite for further intimacy. We had found something we agreed on.

Sleeping with my best friend was a natural progression in the relationship, a new way of knowing intimacy and connection. I was taken back to when I was fifteen and wanting a male's touch and attention, and to an understanding that I wasn't ready to handle sexual intimacy in college. When I was ready and it was right, I made the connection.

We spent the summer together, one that included my birthday celebration on a dinner cruise on Lake Michigan. This was a special event because I usually spent my birthday alone with not a celebratory thing about it. He was a gentleman, something I found attractive, along with his gestures—his hand on the small of my back, searching to put my hand in his, his eyes looking into mine and speaking to me in smiles. The small intimacies were attachments I found comforting, like home. Now that I had a job—even though I was miserable in it—and a boyfriend, I wondered if the two would ever be balanced where the job was just as exciting and challenging as the boyfriend. As it turned out, after that summer, it was the boyfriend who became less exciting and more challenging. Our busyness was no longer mutual. His desire to go out, to even connect with me, waned.

It was a beautiful fall day, and I suggested we take a drive north to the suburbs. "I'll even drive. The day's on me," I said, in an overt attempt to create a fun and pleasant experience.

We got in the car, and I started to drive.

"Have you ever been to Northbrook Court? It's a nice indoor mall with movie theatres and restaurants," I asked. I thought maybe getting out of the city to the suburbs would be a welcome return to when we knew how to be with each other.

I interpreted his lack of response as compliance. Our drive continued without conversation.

"You feeling okay?"

"Yep."

"You look tired. Maybe you'd rather be at home sleeping?"

We parked.

"Maybe I'm not into walking around right now."

"Why didn't you say something before we left? You're always tired. You don't want to do much of anything anymore." I didn't care about the drive, but I did care about his lack of interest in wanting to be with me.

"Maybe we should drive back," he said.

My emotions said this was the start of the end of something I had thought had no ending. Our conversations became more like chats—elevator conversations and weather reports. The whirlwind courtship was changing with the autumn winds and dropping temperatures. It was out of my control; I couldn't make him want to be with me. My happiness was turning to sadness, not for myself because of a selfish attitude, but for Cliff. I felt bad for him that maybe he wanted out but didn't know how to manage it.

As much time as I spent at Cliff's apartment, it not only looked different but also felt different. On a visit during the holidays, I spotted self-help guides and other books referencing relationships stacked on an end table. I interpreted these as evidence of his need to understand relationships and as a signal that ours wasn't for him anymore.

I hadn't seen or spoken to Cliff for a couple of months after that visit, so when he invited me to lunch, I was curious and a little afraid. I didn't know what to expect. This lunch had a purpose, and it wasn't social. Cliff announced he was going away for spring vacation.

"Huh?" I asked.

"I'm going with Janet."

"Your sister, the one I was supposed to meet?"

Silence.

"The time apart will do us good."

Time apart? Do us good? What's that supposed to mean?

"Where's this coming from? What happened?" My voice was raised.

"I just need some time."

I sank back in my seat. Nothing more was said. It was time to leave. Later that day, as I replayed our conversation—or really, the lack of one—in my head, I took his words as definitive. I didn't hear from Cliff while he was away. In fact, I'm not sure when he returned. Several months had passed when he called to ask me to lunch.

We sat next to each other, not opposite, at the table. This seating was comforting, reassuring, as if everything was okay. We ordered and small-talked until we were served. This was my cue to start the real conversation.

"What's up?" I said. My words were optimistic and friendly. *Maybe he has an idea for us to go away for a weekend or a special Saturday night out.*

We were only a few bites into our lunch when Cliff pulled out a small photo album from his pocket and placed it on the table. Together we stared at the book as if it was something to be avoided. I opened the first page to see us on my birthday dinner cruise. I continued to flip through the album to see consistent smiles and sparkles in our eyes, which revealed a couple enjoying shared happiness.

"You took a lot of pictures that day, my birthday . . . those roses . . . and us, and dinner on the deck. What's in the back of here, more photos? I remember when I took these at your apartment when we first met . . . that was a while ago, in the beginning."

I thought this was a thoughtful gesture on his part, one where he offered in his hand happy memories to me.

"Sorry it took me a while, but I wanted to put this together for you. I thought you would want it."

"I do want these pictures. I see how happy I am, how happy we were. That was the best day, the best birthday I ever had. Up until then, I always spent it alone, with nothing to do. But you made it special. And I'm sorry it's still not like that for you. What happened?"

"I just can't make a commitment to you."

As tears welled, I put my head down. I was losing my best friend. He was breaking up with me.

"You always told me to be honest with you about everything, how I was feeling, if things were ever to change, that you would always want to know," he continued.

"Yes, I did," I whispered.

It was time to leave. It was as if all that needed to be said had been put out on the table; the photo album spoke volumes; that was then and this is now. Things had changed. At least we had the memories.

We waited for the check in silence. I grabbed my book and held it tight, as if it were all I had, filled with memories and good feelings. I saw sadness in Cliff's hazel eyes. He watched me while he cradled my arm as we walked through the restaurant and out the door.

I clung to my photos as if to extract elated feelings that were portrayed in the snapshots and infuse them into me. They were glimpses of hope, happiness, and growth in life. It was difficult but affirming to hold my photo book, embracing connections, because I could move forward knowing I was able to experience the nuances in a relationship, just as I knew others did too. I had learned to love someone and, because of it, to let him go.

elle

September. My mind wandered as I sat on the bus on my way to work. *Why doesn't anyone want to be with me? I'm a nice person, I'm smart, I have a job, and I'm self-sufficient.*

My determination to get a new job overwhelmed me, but knowing that my probation had expired made me a nervous wreck because I thought I would be sent out the door at the slightest error in judgment. I was never given any clarity about why I was on probation. But even if I had understood, I believed it would not have made any difference. I was convinced I was going to be fired, and probation was the necessary step they had to take. Trying to read my manager from her actions and the actions of her boss became an obsession. *Are they referencing me with their glances as they talk about me? Are they really watching me?*

I was put to the test one afternoon. United Airlines, my account, had a plane crash. Protocol dictated ads be pulled from all broadcast media. I needed to manage the incident by implementing the procedure, delegating the phone-call load to coordinators, who called broadcast media markets throughout the country to request that ads be pulled. I was marking call sheets and putting them into piles when my manager interrupted.

"What are you . . . why are you . . . This isn't working, this is a crisis and you're not . . ." she said. "We have to start calling now." She grabbed my sheets and ran to the first available coordinator, haphazardly dropping papers on desks.

"A crisis?" I asked. "Am I not working fast enough? I'm getting it done." She picked up a phone at an empty desk and started dialing.

She never did answer my questions. I didn't understand why she thought it a crisis. I questioned whether my manager had been standing in wait during my probation, ready to test my performance if a situation like this erupted. I noticed her observing the two rows of desks manned by a dozen coordinators while I implemented protocol. But I had relinquished my role, and I didn't know where I belonged. My manager had taken over. I stood silent in limbo.

As the calls wound down I sensed the "crisis" was my downfall. I was ready to defend my performance; I had done all the right things, just as I had several times before on one of my accounts. The end result was achieved: not one spot aired, anywhere.

In the late morning of the following day, all four managers filed stiffly out of their offices carrying their papers and ducked into other offices, shutting doors behind them. I continued to clock-watch until noon. The floor had emptied for lunch, and I was called into the head manager's office. Heat spread to my face and radiated throughout my body. I shook inside in anticipation of a confrontation.

"Sit down," Pat said, "and shut the door."

"You've been on probation now for thirty days, and we have been watching your performance. How you handled that crisis yesterday was inexcusable. You didn't handle it effectively, and Lori had to step in."

"Huh . . . crisis?"

"You were . . . a disaster . . . a mess," she continued. She raised her deep smoker's voice while waving a pointed finger in my face. Her furiousness made her stutter.

"You are being terminated. Get your things and leave."

I had my directive in a matter of seconds from a cold, red-faced, angry woman inside the confines of a ten-by-eight office with no window. I was speechless, shocked as I sat and stared at her in this stifling air. I didn't understand why this was happening.

"What does that mean? Why was I a mess? What did I do wrong? Can't we please talk about this?" I pleaded.

"No."

"This isn't right. It's not fair. I've been here three years, each year earning a promotion, and then all of a sudden I get fired? Can't you tell me what I did wrong?" I believed she wanted to hurry me out as quickly as she had dismissed me.

"No more discussion. Go." Her wild-eyed expression revealed her lack of control.

My God, how can she talk to anybody this way? I thought as I walked out of her office, defeated. They had set me up to fail, and no amount of talking through it or understanding my actions would have changed the outcome. I stood immobile, waiting for an elevator, with my head bowed, like a child who had just gotten herself into serious trouble. They made me out to be a bad person, and I needed to leave because I wasn't worthy of working there. The elevator ride to the lobby was slow and deliberate. Unable to breathe, I wanted to get out of there fast, as if on the brink of a panic attack. I stood paralyzed at the corner of Randolph and Michigan as the day's noon rush stirred the lunch-hour workers' brisk pace. Logic advised me to go home, but it was wrong to go home in the middle of the day, so I headed to Cliff's office a couple of blocks north, off Michigan Avenue. I remembered a letter he'd sent me just weeks after we broke up, telling me how sorry he was but reminding me he had been honest. I tapped into the intimacy of that letter when I needed a protector and friend. I believed he still genuinely cared about me because of his continuous, albeit infrequent, calls to me to "see how I was doing."

I walked into his office and looked at him. "I just got fired," I said in a soft tone.

He closed his door. I sat on the couch while he stood in front of me. I started to cry—to wail, was more like it. It wasn't the getting fired part; it was a release of the tension, anxiety, and pressure, as if I were a balloon that had grown larger with each stressful day and had popped, letting go in deflation.

"She talked at me like I was a child," I said.

Cliff sat down next to me.

Silence. Either he was right in the middle of something and distracted and I'd interrupted him, or he didn't know how to handle me.

"Do you want to call someone?" he asked.

I walked over to his desk to call . . . who? Who would I call? I noticed a photo of a dark-haired, heavyset woman in a picture frame on his desk. I stared at her face, then picked it up and showed him.

"Who the hell is this?" I asked. I knew the answer, but I wanted him to feel as bad as I did.

"Maria."

"Who? Oh, I get it. She's the reason you couldn't make a commitment, the reason why you canceled our time, the reason for all those relationship books you are reading. I can't believe this. How much worse can this day get?"

"You said you wanted me to be honest with you, always." He bowed his head, and his eyes stared at the worn carpet. "I wanted to see other people," he said softly.

"This quickly? My God, you already have a picture of her on your desk. You never asked me for my picture. God, unbelievable. I'm leaving. I should never have come here at all. Stupid. Stupid me. Stupid to ever think . . . I just hope you find with Maria what you couldn't with me."

I walked out.

The bus ride home from work at lunchtime on that ominous, gray October day, heading north on Lake Shore Drive, felt like an out-of-body experience. My body was planted numbly on a city bus seat while my mind was still in that office, firing thoughts at the speed of light. I suddenly became tired and cold. I strained to look out the window to meet the familiar corner where my apartment building stood, but I couldn't see anything. Even though dirt, smudges, and oily residue on the window distorted my scenery, I could sense the motion of the lake's waves crashing upon the boulders, giving me my sense of place. I was the reflection of the outside, my skin freckled with goose bumps in the cold and loneliness of that day.

I stood in the center of my studio apartment looking for the familiar in my day of unfamiliarity. I flopped down on the well-worn couch, the heaviness of the day weighing me down, fully compressing the springs to the bottom. I had touched the ground. I stared out the window that afternoon—for what must have been hours—stunned, replaying my conversation with that rude woman in my head, with flash photos of her kinky, fly-away hair as she waved her tightened fist with one finger pointing at me, face reddening, deep voice growing louder, as if I couldn't hear her the first time she told me to leave. They made me out to be a failure and not good enough to be working at Leo Burnett. I had worked long, hard hours, and I cared about my job and the people I worked with. I couldn't rationalize the two opposing views, the one I had come to believe from my college professors, who told me I had what it took to make it, and the other from this unprofessional manager.

I was buzzed with anxiety that I should have done something about what happened, but there wasn't anything to do. I had been programmed at my job and at home with my mother years ago to fix things, to jump in, to manage a situation. This was one I couldn't fix.

From my apartment window, I spotted the usual commuters who disembarked the "L" with me. Their lives were walking in front of me, down below, and I was three flights above, watching them pass. *Where do I fit in?* I bowed my head, pulled my feet to my chest, and rolled up in the center of the couch. I held myself together. I was going through withdrawal where my addiction, my job, had to run out of my veins in order for renewed life blood to course freely so I could become me again. I would gain myself back after growing more thick skin.

The next day, I had this overwhelming compulsion to do something, to busy my idle body and awaken my numbness. Perhaps I could flee, run away from being confronted with deciding what to do next. So I took a walk. I remembered the days of my young girlhood when I'd walked my home's perimeter and any long trek I made thereafter, establishing my footing on solid ground, like dropping anchor to stabilize a drifting vessel. I dressed in warm clothes to protect me from the wind and the damp, cold air. Ambling down the three flights of stairs, I met the empty lobby. I stood outside the front door and surveyed the intersection as if I were trying to find the familiar. This time I had no direction. Which way was I supposed to go? I'd always had a direction when I took my walks, but now I had no plan. Ambling outside in the middle of the afternoon felt odd as I walked east toward the water, as if I had a destination in mind and I was late getting there. I eventually reached the end, the lake. I remembered how the sight of water or being near it brought an unconscious calm to my anxious body. Water was always an attraction for me, whether sitting poolside in my younger years feeling the sun's relaxing effect or walking parallel to Lake Michigan's shore. But now Lake Michigan didn't even look friendly. The high winds made the waves billow and crest until they crashed into the mountainous boulders stacked in an outline. I had been defeated, feeling shattered and limp, just like waves crashing against rocks.

I didn't want to be outside anymore; I didn't belong. I didn't belong in a world where everyone else was working, going to school, or had things to do. I didn't have anything like that to occupy my day; I wasn't busy. I could not find anything to connect to, to find the comfort and safety that is home. I returned to my apartment and collapsed on my bed, staring at the ceiling as if I would find the answer, my guidance, written on it. I squinted to find writing above, but the only thing I found were cracks, some bigger than others, two cobwebs, and mismatched colors of paint. I saw my reflection in the ceiling, the cracks, the mismatches, the old and worn. I wasn't together in full picture.

I rolled over to look at the clock not knowing how long I was idle. Five thirty. I got up to flip on the local TV news. They were calling it Black Monday, a stock market crash that day. Just more drama to add to getting fired, seeing Maria's photo—now the stock market crashing. Could it have gotten any worse? I had no one to talk with except the voices in my head. And then I started to laugh about the ridiculous way the termination had been carried out. My laughter turned to relief because I understood I'd been fired from this job for a reason. I had been stuck in Traffic for three years, wishing, praying to discover a way out, a way up to a better place. My wish had come true, just not exactly the way I had hoped—but I trusted it was the best way. And now I was free.

Yes, my college professor had been right. I did have what it took to be successful. I had gotten my first job out of college at a prestigious ad agency. I'd also been fired by that agency, an agency my school peers could only dream of, because I wanted to advance in my career and continue to be successful, and I could only do that by leaving the agency. Getting fired enabled me to move forward in search of my place to be.

I knew I hadn't done anything wrong. I'd done my best. God didn't let anything bad happen to me.

elle

The unemployed fall months bled into winter days and into the holidays, where I found no cheer. I couldn't succumb to the festivities. My mood matched the bleakness of the gray skies, and my internal temperatures ran as cold as the outside. I was tired. I sold my bike, deferred my student loans, and placed my Garcia Spanish guitar in impeccable condition on consignment. My unemployment insurance just covered my rent and expenses. I was going through my savings. I didn't want to live like this anymore.

One night I couldn't get out of a stupor. I saw my apartment like a dark box with expansive, thick cloudy windows obscuring the outside. My sense of place was shattered as I sat surrounded by dark heaviness exuded by the four cement walls, their boundaries overpowering my desire for strength. I sat on the threadbare shag carpet feeling drafty cold air battling heat from the vents that pushed out plumes of warmth. The dim light and cold pulled me into gray nondescript existence. I felt as if some energy force had taken hold of me, and I was resisting, trying to match the force's strength with my own. I held my breath, twirling in fear and anticipation of when this would be over. I had to ride out the storm and stay grounded, balanced, and headed in a direction only I would determine.

I faced a battle of control. On the one hand, I knew that getting fired and losing direction had been out of my control; on the other, I wanted to stand up, be in control, and direct my own course. The confrontation became too much; I hurt, physically and mentally. Was I in a breakdown or depressive state?

I thought of Len. He had helped me through those difficult times during my Burnett days by being a good listener. Whether it was a night out to a city concert, an Italian dinner, or an invite to his house, he'd tried to comfort me, to distract me from my bouts of depression and frustration from feeling lost, unconnected, and not in a good place. But reaching out to him was a temporary distraction; my discomfort and periodic depressions remained.

The next Saturday he called. Expecting our talk to be about me, I became uncomfortable when the conversation turned to being about us. His interest in me was clearly more than being just a good friend.

"I know you're struggling. I can see it, and I sure can hear it in your voice. But I'm here."

"I know you are, and I'm glad you are."

"And sometimes I get the feeling you don't want me here, like you've put up a wall and I can only get so far before it goes up."

"I don't know what to say. I'm focused on getting a job and finding a good place, to be happy that . . ."

"You wouldn't have to struggle. You could have anything you need."

I knew what he was really saying. He was offering to become a couple. I didn't want to face this discussion; I had too much on my mind.

"I . . . can't . . . do that. I have to be on my own, not dependent. I have to work, to support myself. It's what I need to do . . ." I thought I had hurt his feelings. How would I have felt if someone told me that? Rejected. I wanted to remain as we were—friends. But I would understand if he couldn't.

"Okay, it's okay.

I was relieved at his response. This conversation was a good thing. We could still remain as we were.

My job was looking for a job. My notebook, a combination journal, call list, and tracking system, was my path, my map to moving forward. I remember how Dad used this practice to find a new job after he got let go from Admiral while Tim and I were kids in the Carlisle house. He looked for consulting jobs in the newspaper, meticulously cutting executive ads from the "help wanted" pages of the *Chicago Tribune* and keeping a log as he sent out his résumés and made phone calls. I was reminded that he was still a part of me, that we shared similar ways of going about solving a problem or meeting a challenge—methodical and plotted. Drawing a connection to Dad then, despite my years of believing in our lack of connection, infused me with strength, as if he had just placed his hand on my shoulder in guidance. Just when I dismissed really knowing him, I saw him through our similarities.

I believed I would get closer to getting a job with every résumé mail drop. I made phone calls strategically during the day, asked for informational interviews, and knew to never leave one without getting another contact name. I read everything I could get my hands on, believing that with each *Adweek* article I read and every person I talked to, I would get that much closer to retrieving my sense of belonging and connecting. My diligence and determination just had to pay off.

On a whim and a need for distraction, I drove into the city on a Friday night to see Pat perform. We hadn't spoken or seen each other for many months. I didn't want him to know I was there, but I needed to connect to something I associated with good feelings. After the show, I saw Pat, and then I saw Christine next to him. She was an actress, blonde, petite and young, with a fresh innocence I knew Pat would be attracted to. We locked eyes, studying each other as if we were having a conversation but not saying anything. Christine's head bounced from Pat's face to mine as if she were trying to read the confidential discussion. Pat smiled as he grabbed my hands, leaned in, and kissed me on the cheek. I looked at Christine. Her eyebrows were raised above her wide-eyed expression.

"How are you doing? You all right? I'm really glad to see you," Pat whispered in my ear. I didn't have words to return, but I did have a concentrated look at him invoking memories, grasping my imagination, and leading me into unreality. When Christine excused herself, Pat drew me closer into a dark corner of the bar. "If you ever need money, I could help you out," he said.

"Thanks, I appreciate it. I'll be just fine. Things will work out soon."

I stayed at the nightclub to talk with the other actors. The few hours of diversion enabled me to travel back to happier times.

When the conversations waned, I walked to the door, turned, and looked over my shoulder to see something I had seen many times before. Pat was standing next to four actor friends seated at the bar, where they were in their element. The one standing tall was special. And I remembered the scene and carried it with me as I walked away.

At least I got it all over with at the same time, breaking up, getting fired, depression, not being with Pat. These experiences made impressions, some never forgotten, others faded enough to remember the circumstances of their birth but not their markings. Healing from my experiences with these men and the failure at my job provided a blanket that covered me with an ability to cope. I gained the ability to recognize and celebrate when the smallest of good things were upon me. I reconnected with gratitude, returning to a place of appreciation, a place from which I had strayed but had not forgotten.

conviction

I have always been a voracious reader, but I struggled to find time to read all I wanted. Unemployment gave me the time. I was a follower of columnist George Lazarus on advertising and marketing in the *Chicago Tribune*. George was going to do it for me. I was convinced he was going to give me in his column the name of an ad agency to contact. And he did. He wrote about a new, small agency that was in the process of completing broadcast commercials. I sent a letter to the owner of the agency and positioned myself as someone they needed. This opportunity was going to happen.

My confidence soared when I got a phone call from the agency a week later to ask me to come in for an interview.

After I talked with Tim, account director and agency partner, he escorted me to the owner's front office, where Jan, the agency's owner, sat at a table that was home to stacks of papers in no particular pile or order. As she shouted over the telephone, her frizzy, flyaway red hair matched her distressed look. Her blue eyes; pale, freckled face; and skinny, petite frame didn't fool me. She spoke loudly and bluntly, in a voice that matched her hard edge. I anticipated a meeting that would be the opposite of the one I had with Tim after she ended her phone conversation.

"Do you know anything about bills and estimates? Shouldn't the bills reflect the amounts of the estimates? And just look how over budget this is. Who worked up this production?" Jan demanded. Her fist pounded the table to punctuate her questions.

"Do you know how to reconcile bills, post production?"

"Yes, I believe I could do it."

"Did you talk to Timmy?"

"Yes, I did. I just came from his office."

"Do you have any production experience?"

"No, not directly. My experience has been in trafficking of broadcast commercials . . . when the commercials are done, not while in production." *Do you know who I am or why I'm here?* Her questioning made me think I was there for a different reason.

When I left her office, an exit I'm not sure she even noticed, I wondered if this was the right place for me.

A couple of days later, Tim called. "We'd like to offer you the job.

I accepted the offer.

During the first months on the job, I didn't know what I should be doing, but I'd learned from my previous experience that jumping in and taking control was crucial to keeping my account coordinator job. I was lucky to be there with an opportunity to get everything I could out of it. I smiled, thinking God didn't let anything bad happen to me.

After six months, I started taking on account management work for Tim. I was in control of my direction.

When I stood in my office doorway, I was struck by something that had never occurred to me before. I'd never had an office, and now I had one that even had a window. I saw my large, glass-topped desk sitting on a black X-frame metal stand that looked like an oversized ironing board with two accompanying guest chairs. *Is it all too much? Did I ask for something I wasn't ready for?* But then I reminded myself that my friendly coworkers and my small company contributed to filling my confidence that had emptied to mere drops.

Jan's assistant, Michele, was a bright spot at the agency. We laughed spontaneously because we believed no amount of assistance could help Jan, who was just one of those people who was always frantic, always late, and always yelling. We were the same age, with common interests in advertising and goals to be in a more advanced position than we were currently in. When I asked Michele one day, "What are you doing being an assistant to someone like Jan at an ad agency when you have a master's degree?" The look on her face said it all. "I'm sorry, bad question, bad, bad question. Let's just get some burgers for lunch, can we?" Our uncontrollable laughter broke the awkwardness of the moment, and a friendship was born.

Michele and I followed each other's progress in our careers. But it wasn't all business. Sharing work experiences with a best friend made our challenges less difficult to manage. Our camaraderie eased our professional growing pains. A new best friend and a new job rounded out my optimistic outlook.

I wanted to share my new-job news with Len and show him I had made it to that better place. I wanted him to see that I was no longer that sad, defeated person from the old Burnett days who couldn't enjoy life.

So I called him.

"Hi, it's me. It's been a while. How are you? What's going on with you these days?"

"Working hard. Just got back from Italy from seeing the rellies."

"Oh, yes, I remember you've got a number of relatives over there. So, what's new?"

"Well, I'm getting married. And I'm sure damn happy about this."

The unexpected announcement drew silence from me. My heart raced, and my face flushed with emotion. He wasn't my best friend anymore, and we had never been a couple—so why wouldn't he marry? I was a fool to think he would be there every time I picked up the phone to pacify my neediness. I didn't blame him for giving up his attention to me and moving on.

My focus on a new job was reason to set aside my most valued friendship and accompanying emotions to be dealt with later. In my heart, I ached and mourned a broken connection. Intellectually, I knew I had to move on. And in retrospect I was ready to do so.

Up to this time, I had known I could depend on Len for a listening ear, guidance, and laughter. Even though our communication had diminished over the months, I was reassured knowing he was there should I need him. Once denying his strength and courage and that it was solely up to me to find that within myself, I was now able to admit he was my emotional compass, that his words helped to point me in the right direction.

It was time to leave my 1970s studio apartment in Evanston, a place that held captive jilted memories and a despondent life outlook. I was moving to Lakeview, on the north side of Chicago, to a more modern, chic, convertible studio. I welcomed the promise of four new walls and a safe place to make new memories and a new life.

My apartment on Pine Grove was illuminated by an eastern view toward the lake. When I looked through winter skies to Lake Shore Drive, I saw bare tree limbs like hash marks against the gray canvas of water. In spring, those limbs popped abundant green from sprouting flimsy leaves, and the once-steely lake transformed to a carpet of deep blue and shimmering teal in summer. I recognized the life cycle of these trees. They were my connection, all the way from Carlisle Street. The birch trees confirmed I was in the right spot.

The turning leaves lining Pine Grove marked the start of fall, signaling time for change, for evolving, winding down, hibernating for a while and storing energy. The start of spring foreshadowed summer days, which I usually spent alone. I ambled through my neighborhood streets and people-watched and became curious about what their lives were like, hoping mine one day would be the way theirs appeared. My eyes welled as a shiver came over me, and I suddenly felt cold on a sunny day. I turned the corner and headed east toward the lake with my eye on the beach. I stepped onto the still-cool sand at Oak Street Beach while keeping my focus on the distant horizon. All the regular beachgoers were there, the hardcore city slickers—the women with bikinis barely covering their already-tanned bodies accented with manicures and pedicures polished in bright red; the men's bodies fit and slender and seemingly contradictory, strutting as they walked, shaking their shaggy sun-streaked hair as if they wanted to be seen but wearing dark sunglasses in an effort to be incognito. No one gave me a glance or a hello, so I headed south to the apartment that was my place.

Anxiety and lack of connection wore me like an old overcoat. I thought of the imbalances in my life thus far, as I placed variables of home, job, and a special someone on a scale, eagerly trying to put them in balance. I recalled the inherent energy absorbed from the connections made in my youth, when I would walk my home's foundation, planting footsteps and marking my neighborhood, and now I was doing the same in my mid-twenties, at the beach's lakefront. And so I continued to walk. I had time to spend offering a meditational journey to clear my head and to diminish my troubles.

I walked north to Belmont Harbor to see the boats, large and small, tinkering dockside, their bodies bobbing in the wind, and unsteady ripples of water stopping suddenly as they bumped into their berths. The harbor was a turning point for cars exiting the outer Lake Shore Drive as well as inline skaters, runners, bikers, and then me as well. I was curious about the lives of those who passed me and those I focused on in the distance. I wondered if the people sitting alone on the rocks lakeside were truly alone like me or just by themselves for a time. I turned around at Belmont, headed back north to Addison, then to Waveland Avenue, to the park, the golf course. *The softball players over there; I bet they meet regularly at this time on Saturday.* Those playing golf had something to do for a morning or a whole afternoon partnered with someone else. *How do they spend their days, and is there anybody out there who is by themselves just like me?* I was no longer content with being alone as I had once been long ago. Being alone now meant being lonely.

I reached my apartment. I had traveled in a circle. *Have I come full circle?* My legs were tired, my mind was numb, and my lungs were filled with clean air. I believed this cleansing would give me strength to make it through one more day. And it did. God wasn't going to let anything bad happen to me.

elle

When I received my first review at work, I got the customary raise, but when it came to the actual evaluation of my performance, it was all about what Tom, my account supervisor, *didn't* say.

"Yes, you're doing well," he started. He took a drag of his cigarette, tilting his dirty-blond buzz-cut head back, then blew smoke into the air. *The air is going to fill up soon in this small office with no windows. I hope this is quick and to the point.* "You're highly organized, you've organized me and Tim well, the clients really like you, we let you work with them directly, and it has worked out well. I'm glad they can call you instead of going through me." *Yep, uh-huh. Good. Drag. Blow. Seat shift.* "Tim has appreciated all your help and tries to keep you busy. You've been great in helping accounting to reconcile production and post-production estimates to the bills." *More seat shifting, more puffing, puffing away.* "Keep up the good work."

He didn't make comments, good or bad, about how I performed on specific tasks or whether I was meeting their expectations. I had expected a sharper critique of my performance. Though I welcomed the affirmation that I was doing well, I didn't know where to go from there. Would I be given more account responsibility, since they thought I was succeeding in my current role? Later that week, I would ask for it.

I was ready to move to account management. I had started at the agency as an account coordinator, a position where, among other duties, I kept track of administrative details. I remembered my Burnett days when I reasoned I would have to be at a smaller agency if I wanted to be in account management. I just had to ask for what I wanted.

One morning, I stopped Tim in the hall.

"Tim, I'd like to talk to you about something, if you have a few moments."

"Sure. Let's go," he said, directing me into his office. I smiled as my nervous jitters softened at the sight of him. He looked like a little boy sitting in his father's chair, cushy brown leather enveloping his petite frame. His silence was my cue to start the conversation.

"I've been here a year, working not only broadcast, but also some print and budgeting. I've been learning most aspects of account management. I'd like to move up to assistant account executive."

His pursed lips matched his raised eyebrows. "Well, Tom doesn't need an assistant, but I do. I'll need your help on Glass Works. We can bump you up. The folks at Miles will welcome you," he said. He didn't hesitate with his response.

What just happened? I asked myself.

And then I answered my own question: *I got what I wanted.*

It was late fall, and the office was busy with agency work and holiday planning. The festive mood enhanced a strong work ethic among the employees.

By the following spring, the agency was cutting back on staff. Client account spending was down, and the agency had lost a pitch to a multimillion-dollar account. The summer months dragged with low morale and anticipation of more cuts, perhaps the agency being sold.

The agency let me go in 1989 during one of their cuts. My thick skin was getting thicker, a painful but necessary process of surviving in the agency business and, as I've come to learn, the business of life. I learned how difficult it was for a small ad agency to survive. I was grateful for and valued the eighteen months I worked there.

I didn't make it to my birthday without drama. I was alone and unemployed on my special day, again, and it was like any other day.

three strikes, I'm out

December. Unemployment insurance would run out in February. I sent out a few Christmas cards and took a part-time job at Marshall Field's department store in Water Tower to meet friendly people, keep busy, and be distracted. I enjoyed selling sweaters and casual wear to ladies with too much money and time and helping men put together an outfit for their significant other. I had patience for those who couldn't decide if the blue or white sweater looked best with the black slacks and for those seniors who needed to take things a little more slowly. I noted how this working opportunity came at the right time, when I found that helping others and being productive brought calm to my anxiety and lightness to my depression.

I stayed in contact with a recruitment agency and they to me. Our persistence paid off one February morning, and I smiled, looking up at bright skies as I walked briskly to the bus stop to escape cold winds. I was on my way home after accepting a position at a small PR agency. My eyes filled with tears because I'd gotten a job with only one week left on my unemployment insurance. God had never let anything bad happen to me, and he still didn't. But then, answering phones and handling administration and other tasks for an eight-person, woman-owned firm turned mundane in a matter of weeks. I continued to wait for a return phone call from an advertising agency I had been pursuing.

I missed advertising. I went to the Gold Star Sardine

Bar on Lake Shore Drive after work one day for immediate relief of my anxiety by slipping back into a dynamic world where I was connected to a social extension of the ad agency. All three male partners of the last agency I had worked for were sitting along the bar.

They didn't hesitate to include me in that half circle.

"Do you remember the afternoons here, drinking Taittinger, adding to Jan's bill?" Alan asked. I remembered he had a commanding voice when he presented media strategies to clients. He was as confident in his abilities as he was in securing client signatures. We elbowed each other and nodded as laughter erupted, recalling when we took the afternoon off—or was it that we'd had enough of work for one day and spent the remaining hours in an intimate, dark piano bar drinking champagne? I needed to be in the present moment of the agency, to remind me of reciprocated attention and validation. I wanted back into a dynamic world where it defined me and where I was connected. I wanted home.

Spring bloomed with anticipation of the coming months. The phone call I had been waiting for finally came. My spirit succumbed to the belief that if things were meant to be, they would happen. My confidence leapt when I was liked enough for this advertising agency to hire me. However, in a matter of weeks, my insecurities surfaced, and once again I questioned whether I was proving myself adequately. After a few months, I was back at the same position I couldn't seem to get away from, handling administrative details on accounts, relying on direction from my account manager. Another low-level job. I was discouraged to think I couldn't break that ceiling my head continued to bump against as I tried to move up the ladder. *Is this it? Is this all there is? I thought that working in account management was where I wanted to be. I struggled to get there, but now I don't want it. It's not working out.*

I reasoned I had to let go of the weighty baggage I had accumulated from previous unsuccessful jobs in order to move forward. But I was afraid. I couldn't shake the fear of failing again. There was something about the loneliness of failure that seemed to bowl a strike down the center lane of all my standing pins. I debated in my head if I was going to continue to pursue advertising at another agency or quit the field altogether. After my brain dialogue subsided, I was resigned that advertising was no longer for me.

Most evenings I did not leave the office before seven at night. Actually, I didn't dare leave until my boss did. He was tall and skinny and not much older than me. He was also a dad for the first time, and I attributed his anxiety to sleepless nights. Fits of yelling and finger pointing at his staff became the norm as his pale face turned red. He made his work environment stressful and the tension unbearable. One night was different. It was getting late. He called me into his office.

With his finger pointing at me and my face aglow in red, he shouted, "I've asked you several times to put together a spending analysis, and most times I had to wait for it. I don't understand how it could take someone that long to take information off a floppy disk and put it together with information from a book. Your ineptness is incomprehensible. You're stupid; you can't get things done."

"What? I . . . well . . . first of all, I admit I don't have a strong computer background, especially when it comes to merging charts and numbers. I couldn't find the floppy disc, so I had to recreate the information, and some of it wasn't even there, as I understood it was supposed to be. I didn't realize this job was in computer number crunching. I thought I was hired as an assistant account executive and not a research analyst. I've been working long hours to meet my deadlines . . . I don't understand."

"It doesn't matter anymore. I need someone who can do this. You're fired. Leave now."

"But, maybe we can work this out. I'm not stupid. I haven't even had a consistent place to work, a desk . . . you never knew where to put me. I didn't get this far being . . ."

"Just leave, out, go."

I walked out exhausted, mentally and physically. I picked up my two Marshall Field's shopping bags filled with Field Days shopping specials and left the Merchandise Mart. I got a taxi quickly but then realized it was eight o'clock in the evening. I had done my best. My relief that it was over made me smile about the absurdity of the situation during my cab ride home. Here was this skinny, finger-pointing, hand-waving guy with glasses, getting all worked up, red-faced, angry . . . at . . . me. Why should he be so angry?

I had no tears for yet another firing. First my internal resignation from the business and then termination of my job; it had all worked out. Breaking free of this job and its daily weight of underperforming to my boss's requirements enabled me to look ahead freely to where I wanted to go.

I acknowledged what awaited me the following day: unemployment. Oddly, I didn't care. I'd been through this exercise twice before, which gave me confidence to step into unfamiliar territory again. I was going to be just fine. When I dropped my sense of urgency to get back in the agency world, I let go of my anger, anxiety, and fear, and for inexplicable reasons, I didn't care about what I was going to do. I didn't know where I was going to be, but I was okay with the unknown. I saw it not as something unidentified, but as a new place I would identify with.

Letting go of my drive for a place in an ad agency was the key to unlocking my wellbeing and realizing it was out of my control. Liberation, as well as a belief that my place was forthcoming, took over my mind, enabling me to start job hunting once again. But I soon realized that my lack of belonging to any person or place was the antithesis of my connected self during my college years, and that I still had no idea where to turn or even what I would do. I continued to find my way, my place, my home.

docked

On one of my mind-clearing walks, I took the opportunity to stroll down a long, unmarked driveway. Curious and always open to new forks in the road, I changed course and entered an unassuming, gravel-pocked drive, a welcoming strip to a boat dock mapped at its end. I took a respite on a thick strip of grass that carpeted a hill running in tandem with the driveway. This was my secret place, hidden, set back from the pedestrian and bike paths. This was undiscovered public grassland, yet it was private open space nestled against a boat dock. My spot was there, ready and waiting for me to sit and to mark my presence.

My new spot became a constant; it wouldn't leave me. It teased me with pleasure, and then I would walk away. I embraced its end, when meeting my haven after entering it with hollow feelings and drained spirit. The anchored boats adorned the sidewalk like baubles that soften a straight edge. These weren't just boats; they were expensive yachts, toys with secluded slips for the rich and exclusive. These cruisers stayed for the summer, and hired help cleaning and fixing them was the only action they saw. On a bright day, the sun's reflection off their white bodies made them look pristine and shiny sitting atop the shallow water parked between two skinny, sun-bleached wooden planks. The brightness was difficult to look at, however. I wanted the rays to bleed through my eyes and permeate the windows, which were a constant reflection of my inner soul. I wanted to envelop the sun from the top of my head down to the soles of my feet and grant its healing power to pass through my heart and flow outward.

When I stopped and sat cross-legged on top of the slope, I was free from city noises—screeching kids and adults yelling in frustration in the park behind me as they tried to ignite their barbecues. A fence behind me outlined my isolation and muffled the background noise. While I looked at the yachts and the empty spaces of rippling water, a brush on my back tickled me. I looked over my shoulder and saw small birch trees interspersed to fill a forest of thick-leafed trees. My birch buddies bumped up against their overbearing tree neighbors. I, too, was a tree out of a forest, still able to stand, but needing the rest of my tree family to surround me in support.

I thought of this special spot as I had thought of my birch buddy in its spot. I would pass it when leaving home and acknowledge it when returning. My spot reminded me that I would always have a place to come back to, to moor and be alone until the time was right again to set sail and be led away. I sat quietly, undisturbed, a part of the backdrop I greeted at the end of my walk—one I often took to shake the pesky loneliness and feel the comfort of birch tree sightings patting me on the back.

The fall months blowing in reminded me of that October day when I left Burnett. The memories remained on my skin's surface and were easily awakened. The third round of unemployment was no different from the first. I started to fill a notebook again with appointments, notes, clippings, and correspondence. That was all I had to show for myself. As quickly as I found a small grassy hill tucked at the end of a dock with a view I found soothing, my notebook and my spot became my docking stations. I continued to find my anchoring, my place to be.

I had been let go three times in six years and spent what felt like half that time being unemployed and looking for a job. My job search in my twenties was my disguise for the many routes I had to take to find my place and the person who would be comfortable in her own skin. I wouldn't have traded my blemishes for anything else. Tears shed on the outside matched some on the inside, but they always dried up, and I moved on.

My docking station on the grassy hill allowed me a respite, a temporary place to be tethered while drifting, wandering in lateral directions. But as I moved into my thirties, I would discover that I no longer needed a docking station in the midst of the blossoming opportunities that followed.

a new vocation

A call from a headhunter in November of that year was in my response to an ad in the local paper. My game face kicked in, as I had drive and confidence that weren't negated because of my failure to be in advertising.

The friendly interviewer, a tall, curvy, middle-aged woman in a navy blue suit, invited me to sit at a round conference table. We were a small duo in a large den-like room with soft plaid carpet and upholstered stuffed seating arranged in conversational circles. She was all smiles with red lips and white button earrings peeking out from a short bob haircut.

"I wanted to let you know up front that the job is not with an ad agency. In fact, it doesn't have anything to do with advertising. How are you with that?" the woman asked.

"Fine. I guess it really depends, taking into consideration my skills and experience," I said. I had prepared myself with the typical responses I had made many times before when interviewing for an advertising position. Her failure to use any advertising or agency words caused panic, as I was out of my comfort zone.

"This particular company has an opening for an administrative assistant with potential to move into sales and do some project management, marketing, really an all-around assistant to a manager and sales support staff."

"What type of work is it?"

"It would be working for an international company with a small office here. The department is new, just established, and they need someone who has leadership potential and can do a lot of things and be a team player. Would you be interested in talking with them?"

"Sure." I didn't have anything to lose, and my curiosity was piqued. I admittedly was relieved because I no longer was going to feel pressure to perform and impress an ad agency.

"The company is Bank of America, and they are just down the street on Adams.

"Bank of America? An old friend of mine works there. We've known each other since kindergarten. I wonder if I'll see her."

Would you have any time now to stop over and meet with the regional manager?"

"Now? Well, I guess. Sure." *A bank, really? I'm not so sure about this.*

"Okay, and give us a call when you're done." I stood and walked to the door. "And, oh, Nancy . . . you've got . . . a run in your hose . . . in the back, a long one," she whispered.

"Arrgh. Figures. I'll make a quick stop for a new pair. Things happen." Normally, something as unexpected as this would have made me an anxious bundle of nerves, because only perfection was acceptable in presentation from head to heels for an interview or for just being in public. I could hear my mother's expression of mortification in my head. But I didn't care. My new way of handling an otherwise-upsetting situation was reassuring, and I laughed.

The regional manager at Bank of America looked young with an aw-shucks expression and a smirk that said he had a secret. His dark, charcoal gray suit complemented his white shirt and striped tie underneath. Banker attire. As he escorted me to his office, I surveyed the floor scattered with would-be coworkers, their heads popping above the tops of the dividers. I smiled as if to tell them I was coming and here was their first look.

"You've got a great résumé with lots of experience. Can you tell me about some of it?"

"I did behind-the-scenes work on projects and proposals, assisting AEs . . ."

"Where'd you grow up?"

"Deerfield."

I was immediately at ease with him and our conversation. I was someone beyond just a résumé.

"And went to school at Marquette. That's in . . ."

"Milwaukee."

"You have your degree in journalism?"

"Yes."

"Well, let me tell you what this job is, if I can. I'm not sure if I can, but I'll do my best . . ."

As he went on, his quiet voice and leisurely conversational style lulled me. John was a nice person whom I could never imagine getting mad at anyone, let alone pointing his finger in the rage and illogical speech I was all too familiar with. He also would look more appropriately dressed in old, faded blue jeans hanging loosely from his bony hips and held up by a worn leather belt, maybe with an outstretched T-shirt and work boots, a little dirt under the fingernails too.

"There's someone working here, a friend of mine. Her name is Martha . . ." I said. Though our contact with each other was sporadic, we always knew where the other was working. "We've known each other since kindergarten, went to the same grade school and high school, but parted at college," I continued.

"Oh, yes, for heaven's sake. Her office is . . . well, come with me." I was struck by the coincidence. Not only was the possibility of me working for the same company she did, but also in the same office, on the same floor, just a few feet away.

We walked out of his office down a short corridor to her office to find her absent.

The job came through before Thanksgiving, and I could not have been more thankful. God never did let anything bad happen to me.

On my first day, I waved Martha down as she neared my cubicle. I stood up to greet her.

"I'm working here now! Can you believe it?" I was more excited about seeing an old childhood friend than I was about having a new job, but I quieted down and dampened my animation.

"Oh, hi," she said, in a tone that didn't match mine in enthusiasm. Her flushed cheeks made her look as if she had just come out of a difficult meeting. "Where . . . are you . . . who are you working . . ." she stammered.

"I'm working for John."

"Well, it's good to see you," she said.

"Well, I can see you're busy and need to get going. We'll talk later, huh?"

With a nod of her head, she turned on her heels and was gone, leaving me hopeful that our connection would rekindle later. She was a connection from home, from the beginning, from where I started, where I grew up.

A few weeks later, Len called to ask to meet at the Red Head bar after work for some wine and jazz. I didn't question his invitation but thought how I would really enjoy some fruit of the vine, listening to up-tempo jazz, and talking with a valued friend. I also considered this meeting as closure to the loss of the best friend I had depended on through my most difficult times.

"It's been a while," I said to Len as I struggled to get up on the bar stool. "You know, short legs but with good suspension," I said.

"Oh, the old Chad is here." I remembered he called me this nickname during our light-hearted conversations. He giggled, and so did I. Our shared laughter reunited a friendship that had been on pause but now was continuing.

"How's things?" I asked.

"Good. Just great. But between her job and my travel, we really don't see each other much. Anyway, I've taken a new job, and I'm moving to Florida."

"Really? A good job? This will be good for you?"

"Yep. I'll still be traveling—not like the Burnett days, though."

"That's great. Well . . . by the way . . . I don't think I ever really told you something that has been important to me for a long, long time." I began my confession. "How much I have valued our friendship. And these words from me are overdue and necessary. I was really a mess for a while there. I had no one, so alone, but you were always there for me. You were a great listener. All those long hours of talking on the phone, lunches, everything, all of it. I've never been more grateful . . . you really meant a lot to me then, even . . . though . . . I couldn't . . . reciprocate your feelings, I just couldn't. I loved just the way we were."

"Hey, no, no. Don't think that," he said, waving his hand and shaking his head. He leaned in closer, staring at me head-on, and whispered, "Besides, you know I was in love with you."

What? Oh, God. My cheeks ignited deep pink. I blinked hard. *Was I so blind then?* Those words were shocking for me to hear. No one had fallen, has fallen, or will fall in love with me. I was uncomfortable. I shifted on my stool, smiled, chuckled, all in response to my awkwardness. His declaration sent me back to those years when our conversation turned personal about us.

"I . . . I guess . . . I didn't feel . . ."

"I know, you didn't feel that way about me, and that's okay. It's all okay. I'm fine about it. We've moved on."

I was sad, guilty, or maybe crazy for not walking away from pursuing a career and self-sufficiency to a life with someone who loved me, where I didn't have to work if I didn't want to, to a house in the suburbs with stepchildren to embrace, to living a life . . . I couldn't live. If I tried to explain to him why I couldn't be what he wanted me to be, then what? Would it matter now? He was a best friend, loyal, honest, and a pillar of strength to my emotions. I could never express how much his friendship had meant to me at a time when I was so desperate for meaning and connection.

"I will miss you, this, having some wine, lunch, our phone chats." That's all I could say when I should have been saying more. I wanted to explain myself, to free myself from guilt about why or how I could have walked away from the perfect life I had once yearned for. But when I saw we had found our places together and then separately, it was all okay. I was convinced God had put him there for me, a guardian to communicate solace and optimism at a time when I was depleted of both.

I celebrated in my heart that we had overcome our worries. Moving on, with closure, was the best, most liberating, grown-up feeling I had experienced.

I was at home in mind and heart, with place and person. Disconnections connected.

ello

The end of my journal writing came in January 1992, for reasons I still can't identify. When I read the last entry now, I want to read more:

> *I've been here only a year, and I seem to keep holding on to my days in advertising. I still consider myself from advertising. The creative place was a spark that kept me ignited and made hard work fun. I then went to a place where I felt the exact opposite of where I came from. I'm not a banker; I am not like them. How excited I was to be in advertising. Couldn't I have my advertising with the stability of a bank organization? Maybe I could do it, I think.*

What happened to the rest of my life after that? Where was it? There were no more of my written words and thoughts recorded when they were happening. Then I realized that I didn't need to be close friends with my writing and hold hands to make a connection with something that would give me meaning. I didn't need written words to help me understand or calm me in my fits of anger, sadness, or loneliness, because I didn't have them anymore. I didn't need to write the conversation with my invisible friend to help me get somewhere in life.

And once I believed I was on a good path, I was able to remember days in my early twenties, not with sadness or as hardships, but as necessary markers of personal development where I was able to see how much I had succeeded. Back then I would catch the bus at Addison and the Inner Drive in the morning to head to work, naming each exit as I passed it: Addison, Belmont, Fullerton, North Avenue, Division, Oak Street. Citing each exit in reverse, I counted mile markers as if in a foot race to the get to the finish line—home. During summer weekends, I'd stroll through the park at Waveland with a radio cradled in a beach towel packed in a toted straw bag and find the right spot to sunbathe on large flat boulders stacked along the shore while listening to the announcer call every pitch of the Cubs game. Voices from a radio gave me a conversation to follow; connections to a box blocked out the monologue in my head.

The seasons in Chicago are like yin and yang, or the Cubs and Sox, the Bears and Packers, the mayor and city unions. Wait a few minutes, and the weather could change in an instant. There's nothing like the seasons in Chicago, where forceful winter winds demand attention and gray skies clash with blue-gray water, an exhausting violence. Some inhabitants surrender to the intolerance, moving elsewhere, shaking their heads in resignation to the tension. Not me, though. The winter doldrums break with the arrival of summer when sapphire skies complement the pale green lake. Its waves create a rhythm that blends with the pulsing of my heart, an energizing calm that helps me to discover poise in the imbalances in my life, to find not only my place but also my home.

I was leaving my twenties and taking ten years of experiences with me.

part 5

turning thirty

from windy city to city by the bay

My decision to leave Chicago came without lengthy contemplation. My weary footsteps had once marked every city corner, intersection, and advertising and employment agency during my interviews and job searches. I loved Chicago, yet I couldn't find a place I wanted to be in my city. I had a good job and supportive coworkers, but not a thing was keeping me there; I couldn't think of any good reason to stay. I learned the bank's headquarters were in San Francisco and considered there might be broader opportunities there for me in advertising and marketing. If I couldn't secure a job directly with an advertising department at the bank, I would be okay with any job that would get me to the home office.

After eighteen months working in the Chicago office, my plans to transfer to the bank's headquarters were set, and my boss gave me his blessing.

"But all the way to San Francisco? What are you gonna do at the home office?" Denise, my coworker and good friend asked.

"Similar to what I'm doing here, but I'd like to look into a job using my ad-agency skills and experience." And there I was, back to advertising, yearning for something, anything, to do with it. Previous bad experiences didn't keep me away from where I wanted to belong.

My transfer news hit the office like lightning. I got phone calls and visits from those I worked with and even from those I didn't.

"I'm heading out to San Francisco to work in the head office in a couple of weeks. It's a lateral move, but I hope to work my way into corporate marketing and advertising," I said to Martha in her office.

"Oh, congratulations. They've got a big sales force out there, and it sounds like they'll really need you," she said.

"I've never been there, to San Francisco. Do you think I'll like it?" I was trying to solicit a warm conversation, old friend to old friend, but our brief exchange remained businesslike.

"Definitely," she said. "You'll really enjoy it out there." She didn't elaborate.

I returned to my desk with thoughts focused on long ago, to the days on Carlisle I had spent playing with my pretend sister friend. I admired her confidence in outwitting some of her peers and recognized her hard work and determination to prove herself a success and find her place to be. And there I was, still working toward finding that spot. The discrepancy between us perhaps explained the distance I felt.

"Hi, I hear you're going to the head office in San Francisco," said Jerry, head of the Chicago office. With my head bowed, I hadn't noticed this tall man standing in front of my cubicle.

"I am indeed; I'm leaving at the end of the month."

"No one here has really done that," he said softly, leaning over. My eyes grew wide as my cheeks bloomed red. I thought I had committed a bank violation. "And I'm very glad it's you. You've done great things for this office, for the morale here, and I am grateful and appreciative, and you've only been here a year and a half. Just don't forget about us, will you?"

I had represented Chicago as vice president and then president in consecutive years of the Bank Club at the national bank conferences. I had come a long way from floundering in ad-agency pools to swimming freely where most everyone in the school knew my name. I took to the popularity and reveled in the validation that came at the most opportune time.

Eighteen months was my parking spot. There were similar times when I had parked for a while, remaining in Milwaukee for the summer after college graduation, and the subsequent months living with my mother before I got the Burnett job. I thought how time was on my side whenever I needed it, whether to break from a place and a family I had grown into or succumbing to a male distraction. Parking for bits of idle time made a good recipe for guilt, though; I should have been doing something, but I wasn't. I staved off the "should haves" and replaced them with reflections on where I had come from, where I was currently, and where I envisioned myself. These visions enabled me to string my connections along from college to post college and through to what I would need in the future. I had driven aisles in the lot of advertising agencies to find the best spot, and when I couldn't find the closest, best one, I pulled into one farther from my destination and rested there.

Now that I was leaving Chicago, I had received phone calls expressing goodbyes and good lucks from coworkers with whom I'd never shared words beyond the weather.

In addition to coworkers, I called a male friend to let him know I was leaving Chicago. I had longed for a steady relationship with Doug, but his calls for dates were sporadic, which diminished any hopes of having him as a steady boyfriend. He had better, more consistent friendships with his golfing, concert-going, and bar-hopping buddies. However, he did ask me out to D'Agostino's on Sheffield for an Italian dinner and then to a lookout spot at Montrose Harbor. We sat on the cool grass and shared the view of the Chicago skyline to our south on a warm July night.

I thought if it weren't for him, I would never have had this opportunity to experience my city from a panoramic view. My vision was all-encompassing, seeing all my years in one sweeping vista. I was going to miss what the view represented: the place where I started, my only point of reference, a home. The night skyline painted a wallpapered landscape that I would always be from. Chicago was a city I loved but couldn't live in anymore. I would be in search of a place once again, a place to belong, where new connections were alive and fresh, just as I'd experienced them while perched at Montrose. Taking time to pause in reflection was paying homage to home in reverence and leaving with grace and gratitude.

With a sigh of relief and a comfy feeling like when you walk through the door after being gone awhile, I felt the immediate sights and smells wrap me in familiarity. My vision of the city had softened from the hardened reality—unemployment, mean people, and loneliness—of previous years.

However, my past experiences would remain for a while longer. I couldn't escape the baggage I would be toting on my future travels. It was something that would stay with me; all of my attachments, good and bad, keeping me connected to my old place until I could secure new moorings.

As I focused on the sky's outline of gray-and-brown structures in haphazard shapes and sizes, I thought back to intersections and building entrances where I had once stood in lobbies waiting to be called for interviews. Searching connections to places and people during the unemployment days was never far as I traipsed Michigan Avenue from one job interview to another, empty as the day presented itself—cold winters and raw windy days under the grayest of skies. I had shivered at the bus stop at Waveland under a gray wool coat that was not warm enough and black high-heeled pumps that provided no comfort to my numb feet frozen from the cold. Neither coat nor footwear was right for the weather, but they were appropriate for my two o'clock job interview.

I remember that last day of work when I looked at the lake to my right and saw it void of waves as signs of life. To my left, parks rolled out the welcome mats at their doors while frail trees dotted empty fields, as if their stamina were in jeopardy because of the openness that surrounded them. There were no birch trees. I couldn't see them, or maybe they just weren't there. Fear of the unknown, of what lay ahead, evoked tears for memories of the past and what was yet to come.

During my remaining days in the city, I toured its neighborhoods. I walked to Wrigley Field and bought a Cubs T-shirt and Bears sweatshirt. I walked downtown, to Old Town, through Lincoln Park, Wrigleyville, and then Lake View, and saw the city in a new light, which confirmed it would always be there for me should I decide to return. We said our goodbyes.

In letting go of my city, I anticipated returning one day. I believed the city doors would remain open to me. I never ceased to see a cityscape coming alive in my twenties, when dots of light blinked and shadows shifted against tall buildings with blocks of darkness interspersed by occasional sun dappling the bisecting streets. Lake Michigan's water lapped the rocks on the shoreline, never reaching close enough for me to touch, as if to pull me back into a night's trance of the city mood.

But now I was setting my sights on a new place, and I was on my way there as I continued my journey with faith that God wasn't going to let anything bad happen to me.

ella

I moved to San Francisco in August, a month after I turned thirty. I left my twenties for a city known for its beauty, a place I had never been before. I bought my one-way ticket and didn't feel the need to look over my shoulder. The conversation with my mother was not extraordinary as she responded coolly, "Oh?" So did my brother, when I told him I was moving to San Francisco, only his comment lacked a question mark. I was disappointed and saddened, because I had hoped that time and age would have brought us to be more mindful of one another and the choices we had made with our lives so far. I wanted to share my enthusiasm and excitement for my new opportunities with them, but they did not mirror my feelings. A call to my father, who was still living in South Carolina with his fifth and final wife, yielded a similar response, except he wished me luck and told me to have a good time. All of these responses confirmed that this move had to be a gift to me, a gift reminiscent of when I had moved to Milwaukee for college. The time had come for me to be selfish in living my life.

The morning of my departure, Martha gave me and Mom a ride to O'Hare airport. The trip felt oddly reminiscent of my ride to college—Mom's lack of conversation and Martha's fill-in statements, similar to what Dad would have said.

"So, what time do you get in?" Mom asked.

"Should be two o'clock in the afternoon, your time," I said.

"You gonna call when you get there?" Years ago, this question would have sent me into automatic rebellion; I'd resisted having to report my arrivals as if I were still a kid.

"Sure, I'll call."

Mother acknowledged my acquiescence, nodding with a smile in approval. I noted my assured tone and realized I'd come a long way from childish agitation.

"There's a two-hour time difference between us and the West Coast," Martha said. I think she said this because Mom wasn't sure of the time difference, and I suspect she didn't want to ask. Martha was always good with details, facts, and filling in blank spaces of conversation. I smiled at her sharpness.

"So, you'll be in the city, right?" she asked.

"Yes, the office is at the Embarcadero, and they've got me in a corporate condo. Can you believe it, me, in a condo after coming from five-hundred-square-foot apartments in Chicago?" We chuckled.

"How are you getting there from the airport?" Martha asked.

"My new boss will pick me up. I'm glad for that."

Martha had covered the fact-finding mission as Mom followed our conversation without adding bits of her own.

We sat for a short time at the gate before my row was called. My goodbye was as if I were getting on a bus headed for a fun day with friends, a field trip, and would be back after dark. Considering Mom's feelings, her silence during the car ride while Martha acted as her stand-in in for motherly conversation was an exercise in futility, deflating my strength like a punctured tire on the road. We hugged and said our goodbyes.

I settled into my airplane seat. Buckling up showed I was no longer looking back but braced for forward movement.

"Been this route before?" the man seated next to me asked.

"No . . . actually . . . first time. I'm on a one-way ticket moving to San Francisco."

Hearing my words of declaration made me smile. "One-way" indicated the unusual, when round-trips were routine. I was on an adventure to the unknown.

"Where are you staying?" Tom asked. His sandy-blond hair, tan complexion, and bushy moustache gave him a friendly, attractive appearance.

"A condo on Laguna and Sacramento. Do you know where that is?"

"Yep, I live just a few blocks from there—on Sacramento."

We continued talking intermittently throughout the flight, which made the time in the air pass quickly. Of all the seats on this plane, there had been someone from Chicago sitting next to me, going back to San Francisco. I think God had granted me a new friend to engage in conversation, a distraction, and an assurance that everything was going to be okay as I experienced separation anxiety from the only place I'd known.

The airplane started to descend.

"Here. This is my phone number." He handed me a beverage napkin with the scribbled number. "Gimme a call later on. I'd be glad to show you around." His moustache seemed to wave at me as he smiled.

Sure, I wanted to go out, but I had just met him. Was that a stupid thing to do? I reasoned it was an innocent gesture by someone who was nice to me.

Once I was through the jetway, I spotted my new boss, Gayle, in the waiting crowd. We strolled to baggage claim to collect my suite of suitcases and then headed to the car.

Gayle was in the driver's seat while my passenger eyes were drawn to the new landscape of bumpy, dry, tanned earth, trying to familiarize myself with an unfamiliar skyline. The experience turned into a what-did-I-get-myself-into feeling. I had no sense of orientation, as my innate compass had always centered on Lake Michigan, which was reliably to the east. Now, a bay and an ocean to the west had taken my lake's place.

The whitewashed condo building looked new, and the large lobby was adorned in deep reds, glass, gold, and silver, with a front-desk man officially dressed in uniform and cap. I kept to my boss's heels, dragging the suitcases I had received as a high school graduation present. It was the first time I'd had a reason to use the complete five-piece set of Diane von Furstenbergs. When we entered the apartment, dirty breakfast dishes were set on the dining room table, and a pair of men's dress shoes was parked nearby. "Hello. Anyone here?" my boss said. Whoever was living there hadn't been given notice that another tenant was coming or had chosen to ignore the request to vacate. I chuckled at the unexpected drama as my first introduction to San Francisco. My Chicago self would have panicked at the thought of possibly not having a place to stay and having to find one in an unfamiliar city. Knowing I was not alone but accompanied by my boss reassured me I had a guardian angel who would look after me. I was shown another apartment, uninhabited. It was bigger than my places in Evanston and Pine Grove combined, with a beautiful view of Lafayette Park: two bedrooms, two bathrooms, and a living and dining room. I was overwhelmed; I was being treated well. The view of the park from my living room window provided my connection to the outside as a reference point where I was not alone in a new city but surrounded by the comfort of other living things.

I dropped my luggage; grabbed a map of the city, a pen, and a notebook; and headed across the street to join the locals relaxing on the grassy park hill. I sat in a shady spot and recalled how I got here as I looked around at my neighbors enjoying life. I noticed I wasn't the only one sitting alone. There were others just like me, without a partner. I also recognized what was granting me this filtered shade and protecting me from the California sun—a patch of birch trees. Some were tall and full; others looked like saplings or offshoots of their elders. I was comfortable there, under familiar trees and among single locals. I was off to a good start. Life was truly good.

I decided to call Tom. "Hi, it's Nancy. You met me on the plane from Chicago . . . I think I would like to go out later for dinner, if your offer still stands," I said.

"Oh, you bet. Great. I'll walk over and meet you at

your place, and then we'll walk to dinner; best way to see some of the sights."

What a great, unexpected thing.

We walked, and then we walked more, up and down steep hills from Pacific Heights to North Beach to Coit Tower, weaving through streets teeming with nightlife. I was in good shape, or so I thought, but the hilly hoods of San Francisco were a physical challenge. Fatigue and hunger turned off my sightseeing motivation. It was ten thirty, Chicago time.

We continued our conversation at Joe's on Broadway in North Beach over mounds of family-style spaghetti plopped sloppily in oversized bowls. I never thought pasta could taste so good, so comforting, so satisfying. A sated belly reenergized me. I was happy to be in a new place. I wasn't sure if I would see Tom again, but it didn't matter.

I could not have spent my first day and night in any other way. My boss became my first friend, greeting me when I got off the plane, driving me to where I would be staying, and making sure I had a place to be. Tom was my new pal too, showing me around town and being a true companion. They were my first established connections to my new place.

I had a month to look for an apartment, but I wasn't prepared to see what a $600 rent payment would get me as I circled ads in the paper. Initially I didn't panic, but as the weeks passed, an urgent wave rushed through me. Living in a condo, a spacious place across from Lafayette Park with a doorman, too, was not permanent. Free living would not be free much longer; I had to come down in my real estate expectations. I canvassed the city on foot, tracking apartments in the Marina, Pacific Heights, and Cow Hollow; I even took a bus to the Avenues. I knew I needed at least five hundred square feet for my belongings to fit, but I wasn't prepared for apartments as little as three hundred square feet. *How could anyone live in just three hundred square feet?* I guess if you wanted to call

Telegraph Hill your home, you'd deal with a breadbox for living quarters. The more I walked, the stronger I became. I resolved that I would find a place.

And the more I walked, the hungrier I got. And I found hunger dominating my senses as the culinary fragrances of San Francisco's evening specials seeped out of the restaurants and take-out storefronts that dotted every neighborhood. I hadn't eaten all day that Saturday, and after an exhaustive apartment search on foot, I treated myself to takeout for lunch—or was it an early dinner? I walked up Fillmore and stopped at a small Mexican place for a burrito. This was the biggest, fattest, most stuffed burrito I had ever seen. "I'll get two dinners out of this. Not bad for eight bucks," I remarked, as I justified the expenditure. The anticipation of being refueled by the heavy brown sack cradled in my palms spurred my pace back to the condo. I sat on the carpeted living room floor and made a place setting on the cocktail table, pushing aside the neat stacks my cleaning woman had made of the papers, files, and documents that represented my move and my current position in life. Before I realized it, I'd eaten the whole thing. My eyes dripped tears from laughter, then frustration, and finally from a little loneliness as I collapsed on the floor with a belly full of Mexican cuisine, looking up, the only direction I prayed to be going personally and professionally. Oh, ¡Dios mío!

One day after work during my second week there, I headed out dressed in a Cubs T-shirt and denim shorts in search of a grocery store. But my confidence and my steps came to a halt. I had to ask the doorman for directions. I chuckled at the realization that I had not only a doorman, but also someone who was available to help me find what I was looking for.

Forty-five minutes later, the air turned colder on my way back from the store. I was anxious to get to the top of the hill and then to turn around and view the fog rolling into the bay. This view revealed that I was not in Chicago anymore.

During the weekends, I continued my apartment search for blocks—by foot and bus—from the Bay west to the Avenues. When I was about to quit, an availability popped up at the end of Lombard Street, by the Presidio, in Cow Hollow. On Saturday I went to see the place, walking Lombard Street, which was basking in the late afternoon's sultry sun, the reflections of its whitewashed buildings splashing my face. I stopped to get a lemonade at the corner Walgreens. As I stood to rest, sipping my refreshment, I scanned the street to locate the apartment but could only spot a hotel, a motel, a bar, and a couple of flats. I continued walking. In the last two blocks, when the street turned quiet, veering left just outside the Presidio gates, I lost the sun to shade and found the apartment. A two-story Victorian was set back from the row of flats. The ground-level apartment's entrance was on the other side of a wooden door. I buzzed, and the young female tenant greeted me.

"C'mon in . . . so fast they're sending people over here. Sorry for the mess. My husband just got reassigned to a new base, and we've moved from one big place to a small place, and now we're moving again," she said.

I immediately saw my furniture fitting with room to spare. What a coup! "I'll take it," I said. I walked with renewed energy back to the rental office to put down a deposit and the first month's rent. My savings account had never been so drained. I feared not having enough money to make it, but then I invoked my faith, believing God wouldn't let anything bad happen to me. Just as I thought I was ready to give up for the day and skip the apartment, it all came through, and overwhelming relief hit me. I had a job, and I had an apartment. I was living simply and sparingly, and I loved it. I was grounded with my feet planted, where I would take root and begin to grow.

I was ready to tell Marvin's, the moving company, to deliver what I had in storage. They advised me it was going to take about two weeks; two weeks was a long time. I was granted that time to remain in the condo until my belongings were delivered and I was able to move into my new apartment.

The weeks passed and there was no truck. Finally, a phone call. They'd be there on Friday. After work, I brought a sandwich and a clock radio to fill the deafening silence while I waited. And I waited. They weren't coming. I scribbled a note on the brown paper bag and left it on the front door. I started walking back to my fancy condo on dark Lombard Street. As I was stopped at the light on Fillmore, I saw Marvin's in gigantic letters on a big rig barreling down Lombard on the other side of the street headed to my apartment. My walk back was too long; I would have been unable to meet them in time. I had to wait another day.

I didn't care. Well, I did, because they had my things. My comfortable familiar would soon be with me when bits of my Chicago home mingled with my new San Francisco home. I was seeing how maybe my connections could be strung together and that disconnections were never truly made. When the truck arrived the next day, I had never been more excited to see my personal possessions. My belongings—my home remnants—looked fresh and clean and new and fit right into their respective rooms. I was together, finally, in a new space, out of storage, surrounded by security that had traveled from afar.

I kept busy from Friday night to Sunday night with visits to Fredrickson's Hardware, where I bought paint and shelving for the kitchen. I was overcome with creativity inspired by my new connection. I was the girl who once sat in her walk-in closet as ideas came to me in the comfort of my creative small space. Decades later, my unique place on Lombard Street, a couple blocks from one of the most historical old military bases in the world, spurred inspiration to create a nesting space. I woke up with gratitude. It was mine, surrounding me and saying, "This is your home."

Home by definition had changed. Carlisle with my birch

buddy had been my home, my first point of reference, where I came from and where I grew up, but it wasn't my only one. I learned I could have homes in different locations, Lombard Street and the Presidio, with connections to new friends that were happening quickly.

elle

Once I got my home in order, I was ready to explore my neighborhood, eager to expand my orientation. I wandered my street on weekends and found a few laundromats, a bar, and a restaurant or two. A couple of blocks over on Chestnut Street was the place to go on Saturdays, filled with young people enjoying the social mecca of the Marina. Mathray's was at the end of the street where traffic dwindled and the bustle settled, and my apartment was nearby. I could tell his shop was open, even before I rounded the corner, because I smelled the delicious, clean aroma of fresh cut flowers and blooming foliage. The full bouquet of flowers and colors made me smile. So many choices! Which bouquet I chose for the week depended on how much money I had left. If I didn't have any spare money for flowers, I snuck out to the rear of my apartment to a large, overgrown rose bush and clipped some tiny pink blooms. When I placed the snippets in a tiny vase next to my bedside lamp, my place was complete.

Each weekend I explored farther away from my new apartment and became open to my new world. I hiked in the Presidio, absorbing the scents of the eucalyptus and succumbing to freedom and exploration among the giant redwoods, getting lost in their shadows along narrow paths. A different world churned outside the gates. The glaring sun spotlighted zooming cars and groups of young people walking, shouting, and laughing in animation. I came upon the Palace of Fine Arts, Marina Green, and the Bay. I trekked the Golden Gate Bridge. I wondered if my walking reflected a search for something. I established my footprints, marking my spaces and unearthing my place to be.

As the weeks and my experiences progressed, my sojourns of daily living traveled a bumpy road. Shopping for groceries and doing laundry was a production in stamina. I would dump my loaded laundry bag into my granny cart, both of which I'd had since my Evanston and Chicago days, and set out to find the cheapest laundromat. Safeway, the grocery store, was even more of a hike. But when I stood at checkout, the bay and the Golden Gate Bridge were in view. The sun blasted through blue sky, and water bobbed, sculpting white peaks. I was amused to think I was standing in a grocery checkout with an awesome view. Those thoughts and a smile remained with me. My new life had a different perspective, which made me realize I was a small entity, a dot somewhere in life's unending vista of bay, ocean, and hills. It reminded me of my first impression looking at the park across the street from my living room window. I was a mere addition to the complexities of my new expanded world on the park hill. Moving to this new place, so different from the Midwest and Chicago, was a gift because I valued place and me. I had made a new connection. I was connecting with myself.

My traveling traumas of getting to and from the grocery store and points beyond weren't really that bad. With my cart in tow, I geared down from a walk to a stroll through the Marina and Moscone Park, stopping to watch a basketball game and then a baseball game in the field across the street. The sun on my face warmed my cheeks to pink while I relaxed on the cool grass and inhaled the bay water, noting the tingle of dampness on my skin. I closed my eyes and breathed deeply to fill my lungs and feed my spirit, stopping time to live in the moment and capture the augmenting sensory sounds of clicking bicycle wheels, the whizzing of inline skaters, and the barking of dogs. How rich and full life really was. I just had to stop and tap into it.

I had a new life, where I was starting over with new people who would never know my struggles from the past and never come to know the black cloud over my head which dissipated as I headed west. They would never understand that I had moved away from a life that had weighed me down, kept me on a treadmill running fast but getting nowhere. Here I was getting somewhere. I discovered a strength that was good and learned in gracious ways. My carefree spirit was alive, and all I needed to do was to nudge it along, to encourage it.

Each morning's three-block walk to the bus stop at the Presidio entrance was a delight as crisp air greeted me with the sun sparkling just over the eucalyptus trees to awaken their scent and the dampness drawing out their fragrance. I could smell the effects of the start to a beautiful day. My jerky ride to work on the number forty-one electric bus—down Union Street and up and over hills—ended a half hour later at Sacramento, where the Embarcadero, an impressive four-tower center, awaited me. My office unit sat in a corner with open views. I never put much value on "a view" until I came to San Francisco, where everyone talked about having "a view" like I talked about owning a car. The fact that I was living surrounded by "a view" was just fine with me.

Once again, I had discovered a contented balance between being alone and being at ease in my job. Working with eight other colleagues who pitched in as a team created a friendly, informal workday that mingled business with fellowship.

I usually walked home from work, a forty-five-minute or perhaps an hour journey from downtown, to the wharfs, to Ghirardelli Square, through the park, down Chestnut Street with restaurants lit with tiny white lights sparkling around door frames and miniature trees in pots. Money was tight, and I quickly learned how frugal I could be by waiting until six o'clock to get bagels at Noah's for half price. I relished dinner-making and sat on an only chair that matched a pine folding leaf table, a witness to my life and a holder of items accumulating in autobiography that had traveled with me all the way from Chicago. Remnants held close were from a home far away.

Whether on foot or jerky bus, I was busy with adventure and discovery, traveling through neighborhoods—Chinatown, North Beach, Pacific Heights, and Cow Hollow. Part of my quest to anchor was to connect with others. I studied my peer group, noticing that most women looked alike with their long hair, thin frames, and denim-and-white clothing. They wore black shoes of various styles, their feet anchoring muscular calves. Sweat pants and sweatshirts were the alternative to casual work attire. Flawless faces were free from makeup, unlike mine. I preferred "petite," to "short" when referencing my stature, and I thought my stocky legs supporting thick calves were a Midwestern thing. I dressed up for work with what style I possessed, in the simplistic elegance of a dress or a skirt and jacket defined in complementary colors. "You look so very cosmopolitan," one male coworker told me during my first week on the job. I'm not sure what it meant, but I took it as a compliment.

Our unit was invited to the bank's Christmas party, to be celebrated at a nearby restaurant in the Financial District. This was an invitation I gladly accepted as a way to meet more coworkers, especially those working at the home office. I willingly mixed pleasure with possible business opportunities.

On a slow Friday spring afternoon, I wandered into my coworker's office. Though Susan and I were single and interested in going out and meeting others our age, we never became good friends. Her offers to go shopping, for a walk, or to sit on the Marina Green for a while were more out of sympathy, I think, as she knew I didn't have any new friends. She was kind, and I enjoyed her company. Talking with a female friend was comforting.

From her office, I could see the East Bay hills in detail and the blues of the bay water and sky melding into one another. I lost myself in the serenity and beauty of being here, there, outside. As I stared at the Bay Bridge, squinting because of the bright sun's reflection on the concrete pavement and whitewashed ferry buildings on the pier side of the street, my eyes welled. All I could think was that I was alone in a world where others were busy and I wasn't. I never knew how to answer when someone asked me what my plans were for the weekend. I didn't have any plans. I prayed I would find friends to be with, to go out with, to become part of their world and leave behind my aloneness. I pondered a life I knew I was missing and should be having in my thirties, just like everyone else. But I also loved being in San Francisco. I was a small part of a big world where I struggled to step on for the ride.

Turning thirty meant having the grace and maturity to handle what came my way. I found a home and made it mine. But distractions filled only a part of my weekends, and when I found time standing still, I realized I was alone with nothing but time to fill. I feared the black cloud, dark from my sadness in Chicago, blowing west to San Francisco. I had run away from it once, and though I found temporary refuge in diversions, it was still there, dormant for a while, but breaking ground as I stared out the window at the Bay and East Bay shedding tears.

I wasn't in Chicago anymore. I was in a new city I had taken to immediately, but in time, how happy my new home made me may have been foolish thinking.

not again

After I had been working in San Francisco for a year, my unit merged with another unit in the home office. Faced yet again with the possibility of losing my job, I should have been worried, scared actually, that I would have to navigate a new city in search of work, being one with the fog blankets outside as I replayed scenes of traipsing the streets of Chicago—only these were the streets of San Francisco, and I was calm and confident that I was going to be okay and that God wasn't going to let anything bad happen to me.

The regional manager came from the eleventh floor of headquarters to tell us if we still had a job. As experienced as I was at handling career ups and downs by now, I had to reiterate in my conversational head that I could not stop change, no matter how hard I wished for things to stay as they were, for a little while, anyway. I believed I would have a job. I visualized what my new position would be, who I would be working with, and where I would be. I sent my definitive will out into the stratosphere of positive energy. And it worked.

The RM was a young, married family man who looked as if he were about to explode. His plump face was red, and sweat popped in tiny bubbles from his forehead. His overweight body was in continuous movement, suggesting he was uncomfortable. "I need someone to help me out on the administration side, to help me with the regional management that I can't get to. And I'm going to need a sales support officer. So I would ask that you join the western region in your same capacity but with additional responsibilities of administration support to me," he told me. *Does this mean a promotion? More money?*

My concern was doing support work for a regional manager, which possibly implied long hours and number crunching. Memories of being fired by finger-pointing, waving bosses displaced my relief. *Is it doing his filing? Doesn't he have an administrative assistant?*

I accepted the job and moved to a new, larger cubicle in the headquarters building outside the RM's office, uncertain if the job or where I was located was good or bad. I became his right-hand person.

Deb and Carol, two coworkers, and I became instant friends and each other's support. One of the sales guys and the office funny man, took the three of us out for lunch. But the enjoyable lunch with the funny man backfired. The RM's dance of dashing about the floor started with hovering at my desk, down a few doors to the funny man's office, and then back to his office, but not before stopping at my cubicle first. "Don't ever be gone that long for lunch with Deb and Carol again. There's no one here handling calls." *Could he have said that any louder with his finger wagging in my face?* My eyes popped with surprise and then squinted in anger. "But . . . he took us out, we had to wait for a table, we're back now . . ." And furthermore, I thought in hindsight and wished I could say, *Don't ever wag your finger in my face again, and if you have anything to say to me, please say it behind closed doors.*

What is it with these finger-waving-in-my-face bosses? I wondered.

As I was preparing to leave late one morning for a flight back to Chicago for the holidays, I was sure the RM was purposely holding me up by repeatedly saying, "and one more thing," asking more questions, and requesting my help to catch up for his lost time. Finally I was forced to say, "No, I can't, I have to go *now*." There would be no issue in needing to leave to catch a flight if I were a member of the good-old-boy camaraderie; however, I was a female among the banker gents whose numbers assured their managerial power. Just because I worked directly for a good old boy didn't necessarily mean I was included in the network.

Saying no to my boss was an exercise in growth of my confidence and a leap of faith that I wasn't going to get another finger-wagging reprimand in return; however, I believed the RM thought my assertiveness was a challenge to him. I wanted out; our personalities clashed.

Contrary to an assumed yawn factor during bank sales

conferences in the fall, where sales figures are posted in countless creative ways and sales officers boast of their achievements, I had an opportunity to travel to new destinations for these meetings to meet new people from other bank offices, and to be challenged in a dynamic learning environment. All this helped me to discover and develop more of my interests.

The following spring, there was a move to split the functions of my job and to create new job positions. *What can I do to get this going?* I wrote a report outlining job descriptions and responsibilities with flow charts and graphs. I sat in meetings to answer questions in order to help the head manager understand our jobs and responsibilities better. I made myself known to others with the intent of proving myself so others would want to hire me based on my knowledge and performance on the project.

I believed in me, and in so doing I realized my job did not define me; I had a job, not a career, and that was okay. The division between work and my personal life became clear. I was eager to develop more of me with passions and interests that included the nurturing and connection of friends—contrary to a banker's life, where work life dominated and the personal was secondary.

sliding into place

Unlike the seasons in Chicago, San Francisco's went unrecognized. The change of seasons was subtle for me, with only the calendar months marking their transitions.

January in San Francisco can offer beautiful weather for someone from Chicago. It's chilly, but nothing a few layers of clothing or a jacket can't remedy. Locals would say, "Oh, the rain this time of year! Won't it ever stop?" But I saw the sun and the sky perennially blue. I would read the Sunday paper while sitting on a bed of green grass at the

Palace of Fine Arts with Enya singing softly in my ears from a tape player in hand. The sapphire sky was unobstructed, enabling the sun's warmth to blush pink in my cheeks.

When I walked home from work, the darkness of winter accompanied me. Since I couldn't discern much, if any, of my view along the way, I relied on my senses. I smelled the bay water and heard the lapping of the waves rolling in and clashing against the rocks along Ghirardelli Square. I felt the refreshing cool damp air on my face and was delighted that my skin was being nourished at this time of year instead of exhibiting scaly white patches from the dry Midwest winter. The lights of the Golden Gate and the East Bay bridges were my guide, as dots twinkled against a dark and even darker shaded backdrop. The quiet and serenity was my meditation. My aroused senses kept me company, as I was not alone in darkness but surrounded in gratitude. In discovering more of me, I welcomed the many connections that came with my sensory openness.

In my early thirties, I measured myself against others as I questioned where I should be in life. But all the "shoulds" were not me. I preferred to make my own meals instead of dining out, take my own nature walks close to home instead of traveling to parks. I preferred to watch sailors maneuvering their boats in the bay rather than take control of one myself. I never thought I was missing out. Being alone was a comfort, a triumph I that could do it and be okay. The pieces slid into place like destiny; rough edges found their match. I was in a good place in my head and in my soul. I had a life I loved and renewed confidence that I didn't necessarily need a special someone to fill empty pockets.

I would walk into the Bus Stop, a sports bar, on my way home to my apartment after work. I was comfortable there, my new social gathering place, to watch Chicago sports on television screens suspended from walls. The patrons were young like me, regular regulars, older gents, and groups of businessmen and women who had their usual spots at the bar. The bartenders and bouncers looked out for me; they knew I was alone.

"Your Bears aren't doing well in this game," George said in a deep voice. He was standing next to me as he watched the football game overhead on the television screen.

"Shouldn't you be watching the door or something? Isn't that what they pay you to do?" George laughed more than he really needed to, so I talked over him. He was from Texas, and his belt buckle and cowboy boots told you so.

"Nope. Not on duty. I get to watch TV screens instead of doors today."

"You're for the Bears?" asked a different man standing at the other end of the window. He was skinny, with a mop of brown hair. His thick, tall, dark brown eyebrows almost met in the middle.

"I am, and I'm from Chicago with a good selection of sports teams. Which game are you following?" I asked as I pointed to the four suspended TV screens.

"Detroit."

"Are you from there?"

"No."

"You're not from here, are you?"

"No."

"Okay, then, so where are you from?"

"North Dakota."

I looked hard to locate his blue eyes because they were almost covered by those caterpillars sitting above and behind outdated glasses too big for his narrow face.

I never did think Mike was from California. I found his nonconformance to the fashion statement of the San Francisco preppy male appealing. His jeans and flannel shirt appeared shrunken to fit his frame and were more in style of the Northwoods than Union Street. But then I didn't look like I was from Union Street either with my Midwestern Levi's, hard-soled shoes, and a sweatshirt.

"What are you doing here?" I asked.

"I work here."

"And what do you do?"

"I work for a bank."

Ugh, another banker. The last people I wanted to know were bankers. My track record of making friends with bankers outside work was not good. Advertising remained in my mind and my blood, being one with creative and marketing people who wrote mini-stories to sell products. I was of the advertising side of the brain, not the analytical side.

"I work for a bank, too, but I'm not a banker," I declared.

I reminded myself I had a job and not a career, and that I was no longer driven to be back in advertising among the advertising types, who I thought were the only ones who could be my friends.

One Friday afternoon, at first glance from my desk, I saw an unknown person plodding through, dragging a large duffel bag. *Could that be Lexi?* The holidays were approaching, and she had come from Seattle to see me before I headed to Chicago.

"Hey, you made it."

"Yep, I did."

"How was your trip?" I said.

"Okay, fine, great," she said, catching her breath while looking around to see where she was.

We picked up where we'd left off in college eight years ago. Seeing her was an affirmation of the distance I had come. I didn't see the years that had gone by and all that I had experienced since, but instead I saw my friend, someone I immediately knew, familiar. She was a part of my home, a connection.

With only a few days to visit in San Francisco, Lex and I strolled along Union Street and stopped at the Bus Stop, where she met Mike. Automatically, all three of us were comfortable with each other.

When asked for a restaurant recommendation, Mike

suggested E'Angelo on Chestnut as the best place to go for Italian. Then he asked, "So, what are you doing for Christmas?"

"I'm going to Chicago, but I'll be back that first week in January."

"Maybe when you get back we could have dinner or something," he suggested shyly.

"Oh, that would be great. I'd like that. I'll see you when I get back."

Lex and I left the Bus Stop and headed back to my apartment.

"He's a nice guy. You mean you haven't gone out with him yet?"

"No, I've only seen him a few times, when I've stopped in there. I really don't know him."

"You both seem like you know each other well and you're pretty good friends already."

Mike called me shortly after I got back to ask me to dinner—on Monday, Martin Luther King Jr. holiday. E'Angelo, the restaurant Mike recommended, was a small, bustling Italian place with fragrant house red wine that tasted like the scent of Christmas trees. Their pasta dishes were as authentic as the Italian waiters who served them.

On cue, we bowed our heads, stuck our noses to the glasses' rims, and captured the house wine's bouquet—*yes, it does smell like Christmas trees*. I took a sip.

"So, how long have you been in California?" I asked.

Mike put his glass down, , and hesitated before speaking.

"Oh, I was down the Peninsula for a while and then moved up north."

"And how long have you been in this place on Broadway?" I asked, sipping again.

"Not long, just a few months."

I sipped more as if to mark pauses, allowing Mike to offer more information about himself. My curiosity warranted further question-firing. But he wasn't telling me a whole lot about himself. The more he told me, the more curious I was.

The waiter had appropriate timing. He stopped to take our order. The pause gave me a temporary reason to back off with the questions and consider I was being pushy.

"So . . . you were down the Peninsula?" I held back from sipping to see if he would follow my leading question with an answer.

"I'm actually divorced . . . well, almost. It hasn't come through yet," he said.

Ooohh, okay, now I understand. I drained my wine glass; Mike refilled it.

"I've got a stepson, too."

I didn't push with further questioning. I heeded my internal call to back off, acknowledging this was just a first date with no expectations.

After dinner we walked around the Marina. Being with him was easy. The pending state of his final divorce gave us the reason to initially be two friends who were not from San Francisco and who had come together to share time and to get to know each other. But time gave way to my new way of living—being with someone who was occupying more of my space and time. When my perspective changed, I realized we were really dating.

I had never known dating like this before. In my twenties, my experience of dating was a one-shot wonder where we both enjoyed our evening and each other, sharing compliments, and then I never heard from him again. I was programmed to not really understand the meaning of having a boyfriend but to refer to it as "dating someone." Now, my "dating someone" was driving me to work, making dinner, running errands with me—including a trip to Macy's for a cream-colored silk blouse—all with a sparkle in his eye and a smile on his face. There was no difference with us as "just friends" or "dating." There was no definition for getting to know one another, because exploring who we were to each other as best friends was as much a connection as the natural progression to intimacy.

I was ready to have someone in my life. Mike's waiting period for his divorce to become final gave us a pause to become friends and discover each other separately before we discovered each other together.

Friday afternoons were reserved for weekend planning. Mike immediately assumed the weekend-planner role when he called me at work to discuss what we were going to do.

"Hiya. It's me. Can you leave early at all so we can go to the Wine Bar to start our weekend?"

"No, unfortunately. It would be nice, but I'm here till five, remember. I'm just an underling."

"Okay, no problem. So, where do you want to go eat after that?"

"Not sure. I'm just trying to get through this afternoon."

Mike gave me a ride home from work that afternoon and again started in with the planning.

"So, what's up for this weekend?" Mike asked as I hopped in his car.

"Huh? This weekend? I don't know. I just finished work. I haven't begun to think about this weekend."

"Okay. Well, I thought Saturday, after our errands, we'd drive down to Palo Alto to see my aunt and uncle, and then they'll probably want us to stay for some wine, and then there'd be dinner out and then maybe Sunday, after laundry, of course, we'd take a walk . . ."

"Whoa, wait, hold on. Can we please talk about this a little later? It's too much. You're always planning my weekend. I have no time for myself. You're always in a hurry. I can't be like that. I just can't anymore. Too much!" I yelled.

Silence.

That evening I called him and apologized for the tone, but not the words, when I'd had enough and blurted out my feelings, because I knew instantly I had hurt his. Perhaps this wasn't working out. I was controlled by him. I needed a time-out.

Trying to do too much in too little time with someone dominated my hours. I went from learning to be alone to having a shadow. I wanted to make friends to fill a void I was constantly trying to repel. And now that I had a loyal companion, a new best friend—okay, a boyfriend—I shook my head in disbelief, because I didn't want what I had asked for. I was no longer stopping and taking time to reel in me and my life, but rather time was taking me. The spare time was required to establish where I wanted to be. I needed the solitude and security I found with being home.

It wasn't a bad thing that happened; it was a good thing. I was able to communicate my frustration about my lack of personal time and space. I needed to be in control, perhaps a selfish take on my accustomed solitary ways that were proving difficult to combine with his need for constant togetherness. We were learning about each other and what we needed, and I realized I would not have had the experiences I'd had without him. My anxiety settled when I saw that Mike was not an addition to my life, something I needed to manage and find room for, but was a part of it. I had finally looked into the face of a man who was all I wanted: kind and loyal, calm and supportive. He was living life, and I wanted to do the same—with him.

Even though we were busy with our combined lives, we always took time to take walks. As we strolled through the neighborhood of Pacific Heights, we acknowledged the "for rent" signs and told ourselves we were "just looking" until we found a place where we weren't "just looking" anymore. When we did elect to move in together, I welcomed the ease and comfort that choice brought.

Our new apartment was large with sun shining in all the right rooms. The apartment embraced our combined furnishings as we made it ours, carrying large rolled-up area rugs on our shoulders, with Mike in front and me following, to our parked car at Union Square. Soon, the new mixed with my old furnishings from Chicago, scattered throughout and interspersed with memories of his old home and former married life. But we had the new rugs underneath, touching our feet, connecting us to solid ground, splashing back at us every time we walked into a room.

My new settled living came in my early thirties and offered a respite for me to recognize my life lessons, where each lesson was built upon learning from the previous one. The next one would not present itself until I had learned from its predecessor.

Learning life lessons, however, was different from understanding them. As a young girl, I learned that staying in the house on Carlisle was not forever; as a teen, that my dad would always remain disconnected from me; and as an adult, that faith would enable me to get a job and that nothing bad would happen to me. Understanding the meaning of each particular lesson needed to take time. The understanding owed itself to the years required for evolution, to be massaged, to be absorbed into the stream of life and wisdom.

My Carlisle home had provided a foundation and a classroom to teach me about home as the only place I knew, where I grew up, where I was from—the secure, the safety, the familiar, where neighbors knew your name and where you settled at night in a room that debuted each growing year, surrounded by all that was you. Over the years, I learned to be comfortable in my own skin, and with a home place that was not Carlisle.

My faith remained constant through the years, engaging wisdom and grace, unfolding from many bad wrinkles I experienced through life. I learned to trust. God never did let anything bad happen to me, and because I trusted him, I was never really alone.

And when I had learned and understood all my lessons, I met Mike.

part 6

returning home

like no other tree

Moldings and cornices detailed the whitewashed exterior,
and a grand interior of deep red carpet and black wrought
iron stair railings circled up to each floor at our new apartment building in Pacific Heights. I adored living among
the history of years gone by in this old building. The space
was more than enough for two people, and our combined
furniture didn't fill the living spaces. Mike and I had been
living there for just over a year and half when an unusual
call came from his mother in North Dakota.

"Hi there, what's up?" Mike asked.

"Oh, not too much. I saw Dr. Frank today."

"You did?

"I fell. I'm okay. But everyone said I had to go to the
doctor."

"Well, I'm glad they did. You really okay?"

"Yes, I'm fine," Emma said.

Mike and I let the incident pass but not without keeping it at the front of our thoughts. And after a few weeks, she fell again and went into the hospital.

"It's hard to know what's going on with my mom from here," Mike said.

"It is. Should we move to Chicago? It's closer and maybe easier to get to your mom from there," I asked.

We didn't discuss it further but kept our minds open to the possibility.

I had been working several months with management on creating new positions in our department when the bank started a pilot program in Chicago. The man in charge thanked me for helping him to develop the program and reported with a happy face that Chicago was doing well but needed more help. *Really? Mmmm.*

"There's an opening in the Chicago office for a manager," I explained to Mike. "I think I'd like to take it." We would have to move again.

The timing worked out, and maybe this wasn't just a coincidence. My question had been answered. We were off to Chicago.

It was not a difficult decision for us. I would move first to a temporary corporate apartment, and Mike would stay in San Francisco to look for a job. We spent the next eighteen months traveling to and from both cities for visits. I looked forward to going to San Francisco, to traveling back in time where the memories and the life I had there remained just as real as the life I was making in Chicago. I was torn between the two cities. San Francisco was a gift to me, one that I would always have, one I would cherish with respect and gratitude and a full heart. I did not fear its loss or any other loss because living in both cities was integral to my new sense of value and wellbeing. It was still a part of me and always would be my place.

Even though I fell into a new routine, I didn't really know where I was or even why I was there. Mike wasn't with me and that was okay, though odd. I even had a sense of relief, breathing a little deeper because I was enjoying being on my own again. I was back in the city I loved, but both the city and I had changed. While walking, I noticed my city wrapping around me like an old overcoat, but the years had caused the wearing to fade and to become ill-fitting.

I walked the forty-five minutes to work, north on Clark, and recalled memories of blustery cold winds and snow flurries wrapping around me in an unwelcome embrace. But there was always a comfy feel when I walked into my temporary apartment at the end of the workday, even though I fixed dinner alone and sat on a big couch ready to watch the news on television. Sometimes I would disengage from television land and look around in a daze, wondering how this had happened and where I was. Where was Mike and why wasn't I missing him? I realized I needed this time alone back in my city, to pause in reflection, to retrieve an identity, and to find my footing. I was back in a world that was only mine, a world I had once run away from. And now I returned, knowing it would take me back unconditionally. Meanwhile, back in San Francisco, Mike continued with the monotony of daily living while job hunting.

When it was Mike's turn to visit me in Chicago, we spent our weekend apartment hunting.

"We're not doing too well here with this apartment business," Mike said, staring out the window of my apartment.

"How about that building across the street?"

"Which one?" I got up from the couch and looked out the window.

"That one."

"I thought that was a condo."

"Well, do you think they're open?"

We walked across the street to the apartment and stood in the open office doorway just inside the lobby. We waited until acknowledged by a lady seated at a desk, who

227

was staring down into a paper cyclone, oblivious to our presence. Mike didn't hesitate to disturb her.

"Hi there. Any one-bedroom apartments for rent?"

"I've got a one-bedroom available on a corner," the rental lady said unenthusiastically.

"Well, would you mind if we took a look?" Mike said.

We knew we'd take it upon walking a few feet into the apartment. The corner views ahead caught our attention. The floor plan was open, bright, and welcoming.

"Let's just do it. It's fine, it's across the street, it'll be temporary until you can get here and we can get settled," I whispered to Mike as we walked out of the apartment and waited for the elevator.

Moving day was a day of torment, because not only was I doing it myself, but also the winter winds kicked up in record speed through an already-windy corridor. The windchill factor, which was running ten to twenty degrees below zero, added to my misery. I was caught in gusts of wind, cursing everyone and everything that came before me and this move as I shuttled from the temporary apartment to the new one. *What an accumulation of stuff in just one month!* I was beginning to regret moving back, to getting involved with someone who couldn't be with me to help. I was mad, chapped in the face, and losing my grip on my suitcases. I needed to take a break.

I sat on the floor of my packed apartment to rest between moving runs. I surveyed the empty rooms and I realized I was moving—again—and I was left to handle the work alone. Resentment and anger festered. The phone rang, interrupting my rush of emotion.

"Hello."

"Hi, how are you?" Mike asked.

"Tired, cold, and shaky."

"What? You coming down with something?"

"Coming down with something? Don't you know what today is . . . er, was?"

"Sunday? And I'm not sure. What did I miss?"

I shouted over the phone, "Miss? You don't know what this weekend was for me? How could you forget? Or how could you not even remember? *I just moved!* And what are *you* up to?"

"Watching some football."

"Uh-huh, well, I don't have much more to say. I still have to make a few more trips. I was taking a break because the winds are bad, so much so that a warning has been issued and then there's some snow whipping around too. Get back to your football."

I questioned if he was serious about me. He didn't show me that the day was important enough to him to remember it and feel regret or sympathy for me. Sometimes I doubted he really wanted to move to Chicago because his life, as he knew it, was in California.

That phone call spoke louder words than I ever did in conversation. I stared into empty space and was bombarded by feelings beyond tired, cold, and hungry. I wondered if this was the start of a big change where once again, I would be left alone. The advent of aloneness and the absence of home crept through to my bones, meeting the drafty cold wind traveling across a bare apartment floor. I had no choice but to move on, at least to across the street.

I sank on the bed and took a deep breath. The move was finished. I was in a new place again, alone, and starting over. I didn't know how permanent or temporary this was going to be. I didn't care. I was living one day at a time. That was all I could handle and all I wanted to handle. I became restless and tired and anticipated the next life change to happen.

Mike decided he would move to Chicago without a job. But before I could mentally prepare, another change slid under my apartment door. A notice told me it was time to move again. The building was going condo. I moved three blocks east, still at Huron, but on Wabash.

229

I flew out to San Francisco to meet Mike on Valentine's Day 1995, pack the car, and drive back to Chicago. The thought of driving across the country suggested sedentary hours, the monotony of the car engine's hum, radio banter, and granola nibbling. Yes, the hours were spent as I'd anticipated, but the drive across the country was a better experience than I had expected. Through each charted state, the experience of the open road gave me time to live in the present, to disengage from a place I had made my own and look ahead. I acknowledged the sun's warmth and brightness as a guiding strength to follow to our destination.

Four days later, we pulled up to the front of our new building. The small, convertible apartment, which was a fancy city name for not quite a one-bedroom, was waiting for Mike's arrival. We had views of several building tops, including the overwhelming Merchandise Mart, looking like a giant bookend to the setting sun's rays. But my alone time would soon end. I wanted someone to be a part of my life, to live a life I had envied in others, yet I acknowledged uncertainty hiding in the shadows of my emotions. I had cleared space in the closet and in the bathroom, hoping it was enough. I wanted him to feel that this was his place too. But my fears and "what ifs" diminished as soon as he walked through the door.

Mike walked me to work every day, stopping on the return trip to sit, have coffee, and read the paper. I grew restless with his daily routine, afraid that his motivation to get a job had vanished. But I believed he would find a job due to his methodical and precise job-hunting strategy, working some hours but then giving himself play time to venture around his new city, learning the transit system, the financial district, and where the Cubs played. He ran errands and took care of the apartment. He took care of everything I needed and anything we needed. After a few months and a few interviews, he got a job with a large Chicago bank in a similar capacity as his old position, and I was relieved.

Our urban life was moving along well, and we took advantage of our location. Eating out was a treat, and exploring the city occupied our weekends. We walked south to Grant Park, strolled along the beaches from Oak Street to North Avenue, and visited Lincoln Park Zoo and all the museums in between. We took our time and enjoyed every minute of ourselves and the city's offerings.

In retrospect, I had walked the perimeter of my house on Carlisle, marking my first steps and declaring it home; repeated the pattern in San Francisco, expanding my footing by miles; and finally returned to where I had started, in Chicago. Instinct told me the only way to connect and to feel at home was to walk the earth and thread myself through the forest among the trees where the birth of my first connection was a birch tree.

I was a new resident in my old city. I had been away for three years, enough time for good places in my mind and in my heart to find me. The city did not look as I remembered it, with bone-chilling winters and lonely summer nights in which I felt trapped and not belonging. Upon my return, my continued love for the city was confirmed, only this time, I was free and belonged in a new place.

On Christmas Eve two years later, it was hot and muggy in the apartment from boiling water in pots on the stove top and a heated oven. I was preparing ahead as much Christmas dinner as I could. Mike was sitting on the futon couch watching television and intently trying to keep me up to date on the program. He yelled, "Quick, come here."

"What is it?"

"Sit down a minute."

"What?" I said, annoyed.

Mike showed me a tiny blue box. He opened its top. "Nancy, will you marry me?"

I can't say this was unexpected, as we had shopped for rings that previous fall and knew that our moms, Tim, and Tim's girlfriend were all coming to our apartment for

Christmas. He would have the ring, and we would have our family with us. Asking me to marry him while my mind was occupied with menu planning was fun and most unexpected. I wasn't a twenty-something who required a storybook proposal of skywriting or formal bended knee. My proposal was intimate and comfortably informal. I had grown out of the need to find inner contentment, learned all those years ago because I was alone, and now I had moved on to welcoming a person who made me feel just as content.

Planning our wedding was our mission after the holidays. Matters of who would marry us and how and where we would be married dictated a wedding date, as we realized the availability in the city would be difficult. Just when we were about to give up, we came upon an old gray stone church across from the Hancock building on Michigan Avenue.

"Hello there," Mike said, waving to a woman standing in the church's doorway. "Who can we talk to about getting married in your church?"

"Are you a member?"

"No, we're not. We just recently moved to the city."

"I see, well, that would be me. Why don't you come back later today, about three o'clock, and we can discuss what dates I've got open. I gotta go. I've got a wedding."

I was thirty-five when I married Mike the following September, and I could not have been more ready. We celebrated our wedding in the small chapel, filled with fifty of our friends and relatives. Tim walked me down the short aisle because my dad did not live long enough to see me marry. A month after I moved to San Francisco, Ann called me early one morning to tell me our dad had died and I needed to get on a plane. I repeated, "He died?" It wasn't his death that shocked me. It was realizing that our time was up. There would never be a possibility to connect as father and daughter. Tim's stand-in for Dad was right when walking with Dad would have felt so wrong, my arm through his, intertwined, connected.

I was able to see all who had joined our intimate ceremony. Michele looked beautiful in a long mint-green formal gown, standing by me as my maid of honor, always standing by me since sharing our ad-agency days when we'd calmed our nerves with a burger lunch. Once outside after the ceremony, Mike and I, Michele, and Mike's cousin and best man, Tom, walked north on Michigan Avenue on our way to the Drake Hotel for a luncheon reception, stopping for the photographer's pictures in the meridian among the flowerpots and other foliage.

"Hey, is this a movie or something?" one passerby shouted. Horns honked. People stopped and stared.

I remembered my twenties, the days of crossing those city's corners and intersections in hope of finding a job or maybe calling my date a boyfriend. Now, when I stopped at a street corner, I was on my husband's arm with the John Hancock building looming over me and the Fourth Presbyterian Church, where I'd just gotten married, in my peripheral vision. I had found a place to be. I had returned home.

The changes and moves in my life had all presented opportunities. In the past when I thought I had found home, I had questioned whether it was just a settling place in disguise, only to reveal a change in time, telling me to move elsewhere. And this struggle to feel settled had perpetuated a lack of trust in my future.

Now that I was thirty-five, instead of living my days in the past, as if I were treading on rice paper, I let go. I released what I could not control and diverted my energy to the present, the many times I acknowledged my place, recognizing home through connections of person and place, sound and sight, because it was where I belonged. I had journeyed through the decades trying to seek a way of life I believed I was supposed to have.

Places that shaped me held my stories within the larger

picture of my history. Each of those places held a piece of who I am today. My familiar became where I was, the sum of the parts of my life I had experienced and pieced together from my first start on Carlisle Street, where under the birch tree was truly my first home.

I discovered this quote by German-Swiss poet Hermann Hesse when I began to write this memoir. His words, flowing from tree to God to home, are a sum of my emotions:

For me, trees have always been the most penetrating preachers. I revere them when they live in tribes and families, in forests and groves. And even more I revere them when they stand alone . . . In their highest boughs the world rustles, their roots rest in infinity; but they do not lose themselves there . . . Nothing is holier, nothing is more exemplary than a beautiful, strong tree.

Trees are sanctuaries. Whoever knows how to speak to them, whoever knows how to listen to them, can learn the truth. They do not preach learning and precepts, they preach, undeterred by particulars, the ancient law of life.

A tree says: My strength is trust. I know nothing about my fathers, I know nothing about the thousand children that every year spring out of me. I live out the secret of my seed to the very end, and I care for nothing else. I trust that God is in me. I trust that my labor is holy.

Out of this trust I live.

Home is neither here nor there. Home is within you, or home is nowhere at all.

He wants to be nothing except what he is. That is home. That is happiness.

My birch buddy was my sanctuary. As a young girl, I admired its white papery skin peeling and curling like no other tree in my yard. Its delicate leaves, hanging like slender earrings from twiggy branches, boasted shiny green in summer's health and shriveled brown in fall's hibernation. It was protection from too much sun in summer and allowed a winter's sun to warm me. My special tree was shelter, providing safety from roots to tallest limb, to newborn bunnies.

With every birch tree sighting, a deep breath followed, and in my breath of life, I reaffirmed that everything was going to be all right, that God wouldn't let anything bad happen to me—and he didn't. I trusted.

My home was indeed always with me, as I overcame obstacles and always found a birch tree in the distance. Or did a birch buddy instead find me?

There was something centering, grounded, and calm about knowing I was home.

And standing next to my birch buddy, under the stillness of the leaves overhead and enveloping branches at my side, I would always be centered, grounded, and calm.

epilogue

And so we had our 1947 cottage-style, two-bedroom house in the northern suburbs of Chicago on a heavily tree-lined private road a year after we married. As my husband and I drove home one summer afternoon from Chicago's Lake Shore Drive, I was mesmerized by the lake to my right. The blanket of sunshine turned the water a deep blue with rhythmic waves playing and bumping against the rocks. I missed those days upon my return to the city when I ran along the lakeshore from our apartment on Huron, across Michigan Avenue, down Chicago Avenue to the pedway with lightness in my steps, greeting sunlight, to Lake Michigan. With every curve and distance traveled, I embraced a different perspective, not only on the city but also on me.

I reminisced about the intermissions I'd had in my life, the intervals between periods of development and the paths I had chosen. There was my pause on the steps of the J-school after I completed my last final exam, college graduation when I stayed in Milwaukee, the break from looking for a job once I moved to my mother's, sitting on the hill at Montrose Harbor in Chicago before I left for

San Francisco, parked at my temporary apartment when I moved back from San Francisco—to name just a few interludes. The breaks in time allowed me to reflect and offered a chance for me to organize, recharge, and move forward, determined to get where I wanted to be. Perhaps it was my way of liberating my emotions to muster a strong will to get me on my way once again, to connect me to the other side, where my sense of worth and identity would have miles yet to travel. I was reminded I would not take the present moments for granted and, in a larger perspective, take nothing about my life for granted. Through the decades, I was finding the person I was meant to be and defining myself through others or through my surroundings. I learned lessons in difficult ways, but in the outcome, God never did let anything bad happen to me.

I will remember when Mom, Tim, and I were together and connected in every sense of home. It was September, just after a rehearsal dinner before my wedding, and a warm breeze off the lake matched the evening's temperature. We started walking with the wind at our backs and ended at an unlikely place, a couple of blocks east of Michigan Avenue on the corner of Chicago and Huron. We had stopped and loitered on the corner in front of the White Hen when time seemed to have stood still. All of us were talking at the same time, sharing stories from when Tim and I were young, and Mom filling in the gaps of our memories. We had been apart for so long, living separate existences, making decisions without the benefits of family guidance or support. But here we were together, not feeling the many years we had lived separately but now living years in unison. Our continuous laughter was the familiar. I don't remember what sustained the humor, but I do remember Mom had stopped first on the corner in a fit of gut-tightening silliness. Tim and I followed, bumbling along, drunk on the spontaneous laughter.

For that short time, the three of us had an unspoken

bond where our early years of growing up were exposed. We had grown up. I was getting married. Tim would soon follow. Mom continued to be alone, but I was back in the city, a place of history and memories from long ago for Mom, a foreign land for Tim. It was an unlikely gathering where we weren't alone, but together, laughing the past away and enjoying the present moments of each other.

I wish for a more perfect world in which my brother and I are closer; he is not far away but has a life a great distance from mine. I hope my mother finds happiness and acceptance of herself. But my wishes are private, and I believe that someday their hopes will come true. I remember the struggles of my twenties and the triumphs and joys in my thirties. Now that I have finished my forties, a new-found wisdom flushes over me that says I would never have changed anything in my life. I am what I am today because of the decades past, the connections made and broken and then reformed in person and place.

My house now is a stop along the way to learning lessons that were destined for me. I have painted walls and drawn pictures, baked goods and sewn curtains, turned someone else's house into my home with my thoughts and my learned lessons bound within four walls. My world is my home in all that I've learned.

I am dictating these words from a perch overlooking a valley reminiscent of days spent in Anderson Valley, California, where vineyards unfurl along hillsides in Mendocino. The air is still and damp with the sun bleeding through a morning calm awakening every creature. Stately trees surround me, and my eyes wander as though in a maze, starting at the center, through twists and turns, working my way out to freedom. There is nothing more comforting than to see the tall birch tree through my window. I look through the framed glass, capturing every detail as my eyes embrace the peeling white bark, the hummingbirds hovering over the tips of the flower bed, the sparkling dewy grass growing as fast as the eye can witness, and the dark shadows cast from divots in the lawn. Squirrels trapeze from tree to tree, connecting dots and creating sharp angles with every leap they make. The rabbits stir with their mother keeping watch, and the bunny brood peeks slowly out of their nest in the hole within the surrounding curb of the birch tree. They are still so as not to attract attention. I watch and then continue with my work, soon to tire as my thoughts drift. A final glance through my window shows the bunnies scampering to new places and new homes in freedom. They go untouched and are left alone where their mother and nest is left behind. The seasons dawn, the decades come to an end, and the bunnies are forced out of their home before their time but bound for great things and new adventures.

When I was younger I could remember anything, whether it happened or not; but I am getting old, and soon I shall remember only the latter.
— Mark Twain: A Biography

acknowledgments

I had autobiography; I wanted memoir.

Fifteen years ago, I started writing a story that was more chronology filled with events and less complete with experiences of reflections and takeaways. I avoided working those pages, throwing the manuscript into a drawer and hoping the time for incubation would turn it around but neither the book's resting place nor its gestation resulted in my favor. My manuscript and I were stuck. In 2005, I threw caution to the wind and submitted the bundle to a professional for its first, virginal critique. My thanks to John M. Daniel for giving me the most thorough editorial analysis that became the backbone and impetus to my future rewrites. Three years later and more rewrites, I needed to see if I was on the right track–steering away from autobiography.

Thank you, Marcia Trahan, for providing your first manuscript critique summary in 2008 telling me I needed to engage my reader and write a story that answers the question of "who cares?" The answer to this guided me through every subsequent rewrite. I had seen my progress toward my memoir goal when your subsequent critique of 2013 blessed me with your words saying I, indeed, had a story. But I still had a way to go before I could claim my story a memoir.

After intensive self-study on the craft of writing memoir and rewriting my manuscript, I turned to Brooke Warner for help. Thank you, Brooke, for leading me to develop strong memoir, for pulling me back from straying from my theme and showing me how to mend my splintered through-threads with a solid critique granting me my "aha" moments. Your suggestion for a developmental edit with Annie Tucker broke the gates that were holding me back from discovering the memoir it was meant to be. Thanks, Annie, for your embedded questions, prompting me to think and to answer as a memoir writer.

And with sincere gratitude, I thank my project manager, Cait Levin, for working your magic during the book-making process and the entire team at She Writes Press for accepting *Under the Birch Tree*.

I got my memoir!

A special thank you to my husband, Mike, who knew all along I had something to say, who was patient and supportive in pursuing my journey, this dream, of one day publishing my book and sharing it with those who also seek to discover connections, their place to be, to find their home.

about the author

NANCY CHADWICK grew up in a north suburb of Chicago. After receiving a Journalism degree at Marquette University, she got her first job at Leo Burnett advertising agency in Chicago. After ten years there, she couldn't get to where she wanted to be in the ad agency business, so she reinvented herself and turned to the banking industry. Then, after another ten years, she realized she wasn't a banker—so she quit and started to write, finding inspiration from her years in Chicago and San Francisco. Her essay "I Called You a Memoir" appears in *The Magic of Memoir, Inspiration for the Writing Journey*. She and her husband enjoy traveling, cooking fine dinners, and chasing their beagles in circles.

www.nancychadwickauthor.com

Author photo © Cassandra Rodgers

selected titles from she writes press

She Writes Press is an independent publishing company founded to serve women writers everywhere.
Visit us at www.shewritespress.com.

The Sportscaster's Daughter: A Memoir by Cindi Michael. $16.95, 978-1-63152-107-2. Despite being disowned by her father—sportscaster George Michael, said to be the man who inspired ESPN's SportsCenter—Cindi Michael manages financially and heals emotionally, ultimately finding confidence from within.

Blue Apple Switchback: A Memoir by Carrie Highley. $16.95, 978-1-63152-037-2. At age forty, Carrie Highley finally decided to take on the biggest switchback of her life: upon her bicycle, and with the help of her mentor's wisdom, she shed everything she was taught to believe as a young lady growing up in the South—and made a choice to be true to herself and everyone else around her.

Accidental Soldier: A Memoir of Service and Sacrifice in the Israel Defense Forces by Dorit Sasson. $17.95, 978-1-63152-035-8. When nineteen-year-old Dorit Sasson realized she had no choice but to distance herself from her neurotic, worrywart of a mother in order to become her own person, she volunteered for the Israel Defense Forces—and found her path to freedom.

Rethinking Possible: A Memoir of Resilience by Rebecca Faye Smith Galli. $16.95, 978-1-63152-220-8. After her brother's devastatingly young death tears her world apart, Becky Galli embarks upon a quest to recreate the sense of family she's lost—and learns about healing and the transformational power of love over loss along the way.

Veronica's Grave: A Daughter's Memoir by Barbara Bracht Donsky. $16.95, 978-1-63152-074-7. A loss and coming-of-age story that follows young Barbara Bracht as she struggles to comprehend the sudden disappearance and death of her mother and cope with a blue-collar father intent upon erasing her mother's memory.